the **826 Quarterly**

AN 826 VALENCIA ORIGINAL
Published June 2013
as the seventeenth edition of the *826 Quarterly*
Created by all hands on deck at 826 Valencia

826 Valencia Street
San Francisco, California 94110
826valencia.org

Copyright © 2013 826 Valencia
All rights reserved by 826 Valencia and the authors

EDITORS Emilie Coulson and Molly Parent
EDITORIAL ASSISTANT John Gibbs
ART DIRECTOR María Inés Montes
BOOK DESIGNER Lucy Kirchner
ILLUSTRATOR Angela Dominguez
COPY EDITOR Will Georgantas

PLEASE VISIT:
The Pirate Store at 826
826valencia.org/store

ISBN 978-1-934750-37-7
Printed in the USA by Thomson-Shore
Distributed by Publishers Group West

TENTH ANNIVERSARY EDITION

the 826 Quarterly

VOLUME 17 ✶ *2002–2012*

*Published seventeen times a decade, at least.

Contents

Introduction · DAVE EGGERS & NÍNIVE CALEGARI … X
Foreword · LEMONY SNICKET … XIV

2003
Introduction · SOFIA MARQUEZ … XVIII
The President Needs $14 Trillion—and Fast! · MARNIE HATCH'S TENTH-GRADE CLASS … 2
Scraggly, Gray-Carpeted Suburban House · PHOEBE S. MORGAN … 5
That's a Horse Book of a Different Color · CARMEN DEMARTIS … 13
Poems · MADELEINE CONANAN … 19
Please Remember to Suck Off His Finger with a High-Powered Vacuum · KEVIN FEENEY … 21

2004
Introduction · VANESSA PEREZ … 24
Hill · SIOBHAN WILLING … 26
The Feminist Queen · CARSON EVERETT … 27
The Mountain Patch-Nose Snake · JAKE WATTERS … 34
Untitled · RADFORD LEUNG … 39

2005
Introduction · SABRINA YERENA … 40
Dust-Silk Pouch · SALLY MAO … 42
Quarterback'n · VINCENT CHAO … 47
The Fabulous, Stupendous, Spectacular, Absolutely Excellent Day · ROISIN McLAUGHLIN, JOELLE PARK, SHANNON GARCIA … 51
The Traveler Who Came from "The Paris of the Orient" · YAN RAN TAO … 52

Eight Ways to Get an Amusement Park · DANIEL ILLIG 56
Shaking Man · SACHIEL FREGRIC NUNAZ MICHAEL ROSEN 57

2006

Introduction · MYLES CRAWFORD 58
My Great Dinner Party · ELLIOT TAM 60
A Hat · SABINE DAHI 61
The Secret of Blockbuster Hits · GUILLERMO GONZALEZ 62
The Case of the Sparkly Pink Hello Kitty Pen · EMILY MAYER 65

2007

Introduction · SANTIAGO DELGADO 68
Magnetism · JUSTINE DRENNAN 70
Martin Luther King, Jr. Day · EVAN GREENWALD 72
Alcatraz · DAISY GUZMAN 74
Maccanik's Adventures · ANTHONY HERNANDEZ 75
Bullet Points · SIMONE CREW 77
Turtles Inside · ERICA KUNISAKI 79
Warm/Cold (The Sun, Orange Juice, Ice Chips) · MAYA GOLDBERG-SAFIR 80

2008

Introduction · GUISEPPE PACHECO 84
Suit · CHARLIE GEBHARDT 86
Is a Photograph Worth a Thousand Words? · BO YAN MORAN 98
In a Delicate Hand · CHLOE VILLEGAS 101

2009

Introduction · MARCO PONCE 102
Cosmic List · KENNY DZIB 104
Thanks & Have Fun Running the Country · YOSELIN MARTINEZ, JONATHAN PINEDA, MARCO PONCE, DIANA PEREZ 106
I'm from Myself · ZOE KAMIL 110

2010

Introduction · ERICKSON MARTINEZ 112
Wednesday · GINA CARGAS 114

2,000 Years in the Future • JULIAN KLEPPE	120
The Week of the Day • VERONICA SUAREZ-LOPEZ	122
Shalhoubing • PAOLO YUMOL	124
The Inside of My Mother's Life • AARYN BAKER	127
Outrage of the Pupusa • PABLO BARRERA	129

2011

Introduction • EDUARDO DELGADO	130
Letter to Malia and Sasha Obama • OCEANO PETTIFORD	132
Considering Spies • EVA MELIN-GOMPPER	134
For Girlz Who Have Considered Jumping Like Walking Is Too Much • LLUVIA QUINTERO	136
Escape • TIULI KULISHI	137
Not Your Regular Mermaid Article • AVA LYNCH	139
Girls • JUAN SALAZAR ROMERO	141
I Used to Have a Dog • KAROLINA OCHOA	142
DREAM: The DREAM Act • EMANUEL FLORES	143
To Shakespeare or Not to Shakespeare • OLIVIA SCOTT	145
Electro's Diary Entry • DONTRELL HARDEN	147

2012

Introduction • JESSICA BERRIOS	148
Conversations with Walmart Cat • LUCIE PEREIRA	150
Cuties with Prosthetics • CALISTA NICHOLSON	155
Dear Dead People • JUAN BENITEZ	157
Love Blah, Blah, Blah • JACKY CARRILLO	158
Darkness Helping • JESSICA BERRIOS	160
Small Town Loves (Two Monologues) • ARTY ZHANG	162
Cake Me Up • ELLESSE GUTIERREZ	165
Latina Girl from the Mission • ALEJANDRA MARTINEZ	166
When I'm Eighty • URIEL DELGADO	169

About 826 Valencia

The People of 826 Valencia	172
The Programs of 826 Valencia	174
The Publications of 826 Valencia	176
The Store at 826 Valencia	182

Introduction

DAVE EGGERS & NÍNIVE CALEGARI ✳ *Founders*
826 Valencia

Ten years just doesn't describe it. These hundreds of pages don't do it justice.

Or rather, they certainly do the concept of 826 Valencia justice, in that these pages represent some of the best writing done by students at 826 in the last ten years. But when you think about just how much work has been produced by students in that time, it's almost too much to wrap your head around, let alone collect or distill.

Here's a stab at some numbers: Almost every day, a public school class comes into 826 Valencia for a field trip and produces a story together. So that's about 150 stories a year and, over ten years, 1,500 field-trip stories. We also produce a student newspaper, the *Straight Up News,* and that's produced about 200 stories over the years. And there's *Slick,* our student magazine. And *The Valencia Bay-Farer,* another student newspaper, with 300 or so stories. And every year there's a book produced in conjunction with a local high school—another 500 stories. And then there are the countless zines, chapbooks, and assignments completed for workshops. That's another 1,000 or so pieces produced every year. Added up, the young voices who have come through 826 Valencia's doors have produced

100,000 or so stories, poems, plays, books, posters, and short films.

It's a testament to how badly kids want to write. They need to get this stuff out of their heads and onto the page. They are virtually bursting with ideas, with the urge to express themselves.

And we give them that chance. And just as important, we give them an audience. We hold student readings. We publish their work in professional-quality publications like this. And we get their voices heard around the world.

Here's a good example: When President Obama was elected, there was rejoicing in San Francisco generally, and in the Mission District specifically. The celebration was so large on Valencia Street, for example, that the street was peaceably closed down by police to allow for spontaneous parades and merrymaking.

The students of 826 Valencia joined in, and were so moved and inspired by Obama that they began writing letters to him. We decided to collect these letters in a book called *Thanks and Have Fun Running the Country*. We sent the letters to the *New York Times,* who dedicated a full page to them. And all along, we told the students that we had a pretty good feeling that the president himself might read their letters.

Did we know this for sure? Well, no. But we had a feeling. And because we've been able to establish a platform for student voices, and we've been able to get student voices heard at City Hall, and in the White House, and all over the Web, and in the *San Francisco Chronicle*, we knew we at least had a shot at getting these letters to President Obama.

And one day, we saw a picture online. It showed the president getting out of a car, on the tarmac, about to board *Air Force One*. And in his hand we saw something very interesting. He was reading the page of our students' letters published in the *New York Times*! It was clear as day.

So we showed this photo to the students, who did one of two things: They were either dumbfounded, or they acted like they expected it all along. "Of course the president listens to us!" they seemed to say. What kind of president would he be if he wasn't listening to the youth of America?

This is what 826 Valencia is about. We enable student voices to be heard—whether it's working one-on-one with them to polish their work, or bringing their voices to the highest levels of American society.

In between there is much work, and much of it is less glamorous. Much of it is simply a bunch of kids, some of them just gaining mastery of the language, talking about what they want to say. What they feel about their lives—its mysteries and frustrations. For so many young people living in the city, life can be chaotic. There are so many factors out of their control. There are dangers, there is upheaval, there is ugliness, there are winds that blow them off track.

But on the page, they have ownership, control, and mastery. They can tell a story, write a poem or play, and they can feel that there, at least, in black and white, there is order, and beauty, and they can encompass the world and put their name on it.

All of this would be impossible without the thousands of volunteers who work, daily and tirelessly, to improve the students' ability to express themselves with clarity and confidence. These tutors come from every walk of life, from retired educators to bank managers to advertising copy writers to graduate students, and they make 826 Valencia, and the greater opportunities available to the students of San Francisco, possible.

And there is the staff of 826. These are some of the hardest working, most creative, scrappy, and indefatigable people on earth. They have always been a skeleton crew, tasked with doing so much with so few, and they have done more than anyone could have expected or imagined.

We salute and thank, too, the teachers of the Bay Area, for whom 826 Valencia was created—we designed ourselves to assist in making the dreams of public school teachers possible—and whom we thank for bringing us into their classrooms and lives. We love you guys.

Thank you to our donors, who have been with us from the start and who have never wavered in their support. Thank you to our board members past and present—never has so much been asked of a board! And thank you to the parents who have entrusted us with their children and with making their children's voices clear and loud.

And most of all, this book is dedicated to those voices. We have been honored, for ten years, to be among the first to hear these voices. The electric feeling of hearing a young person's voice emerge, first tentative, first unsure, then soon, with nurturing and validation, confident, and bold, and lyrical, and playful, and able to open doors, and create opportunities, and make these students feel less alone, and more empowered, and more able to succeed in every aspect of life—we have been honored to be witness to all this, every day for ten years.

Thank you—

Dave Eggers
Nínive Calegari

Foreword

LEMONY SNICKET

This book marks the tenth anniversary of the *826 Quarterly*. A decade! Ten years! Three thousand something-something days! I sit at my desk and try to think of what the world was like back in 2003. It seems to me, for instance, that ten years ago automobiles had not yet been invented, or perhaps they had been invented but you didn't see them around much, except on roads, highways, and parking lots. And garages. There were hardly any Thai restaurants, at least on this particular street I'm thinking of, and now there is one, which has been there for many years—perhaps ten, come to think of it. Ten years ago, e-mails were all delivered by hand, unless I'm mistaken. I definitely remember someone coming to my house and giving me something. Ten years ago, there was a craze for a particular kind of clothing, if memory serves, or for saying a certain phrase out loud in a certain way that was guaranteed to make someone laugh, or perhaps just smile. Now the clothing is different, and people are saying something else instead. I must admit I have not been paying particularly close attention.

You haven't either. While a generation of young writers, urged on by the noble volunteers at various 826 locations, have been spinning wonderful tales, constructing elegant verses, and embarking on other exciting literary adventures collected here in these pages, you probably haven't done anything nearly as interesting, have you? Well, *have you?*

Rather than answering me out loud and risk looking foolish shouting at a book, why not take a handy and informative quiz? Stack up your own accomplishments next to the triumphs of the young writers gathered in this *Quarterly*, and see who has triumphed over the past ten years and who has squandered their time thinking about something over and over that does not matter in this world or the next, such as how long a Thai restaurant has been in business on a particular street. Maybe eleven years. It doesn't matter. Grab a pen, pencil, or tube of lipstick and circle the best-fitting answer to the questions I have hastily devised below.

1. In 2003, you
a. wrote a poem titled "Rubber Band," which ends with the line "When will this catastrophe end?"
b. walked into the kitchen for no particular reason and ate an apple or something.

2. In 2004, you
a. composed an homage to a famed Edgar Allan Poe story featuring a crinkly sandwich wrapper.
b. listened to a song you liked two times in a row.

3. In 2005, you
a. devised the startling sentence "My puppy (that I don't have) will wake me up."
b. sent an e-mail that said something like "Great, see you then."

4. In 2006, you
a. were eight years old and yet still wrote a poem that easily could have been mistaken for the work of Gertrude Stein.
b. were some other age and yet found yourself tapping a pen or pencil on a table for no good reason.

5. In 2007, you
a. found the perfect metaphor connecting famed electronics pioneer Nikola Tesla and young love.

b. left your house and immediately went back inside because you forgot something.

6. In 2008, you
a. attended a Summer Writing Camp and greatly impressed your colleagues with an experimental prose poem beginning "My life began when I tried your cereal."
b. stood in line for something that wasn't fun.

7. In 2009, you
a. wrote a cosmic list.
b. wrote a grocery list and bought some groceries at a grocery store and put them in a grocery bag.

8. In 2010, you
a. finished your short story about a bloodthirsty mayor.
b. said "What?" to someone who asked you a question, so then they had to repeat themselves, even though you actually heard the question perfectly well the first time.

9. In 2011, you
a. corresponded with members of the first family.
b. argued with someone about something that was almost entirely meaningless, just because you were in a bad mood.

10. In 2012, you
a. were associated with a literary effort titled "Cuties with Prosthetics."
b. changed your shirt even though the shirt you had on before was perfectly fine.

11. In 2013, you
a. continued the inspiring and dynamic tradition at 826 by volunteering, donating, or otherwise participating in a program that is simultaneously improving the world in verifiable, specific ways and providing entertainment for anyone who likes to read something surprising.
b. sat at your desk and honestly tried to remember the first time you went to a particular Thai restaurant, even though no one else but you is at all interested in that, and you aren't

really, either, it's just that it popped into your head and it won't go away and you're even working it, several times, into an introduction you're writing.

Give yourself one point for each time you chose Answer A, and zero points for each time you chose Answer B, and assess yourself using the score chart below:

0 points You have wasted the last ten years of your life, unlike the exciting young writers at 826.

1-3 points You may have done the occasional interesting thing, but unlike the exciting young writers at 826, you are for the most part unproductive and dull.

4-6 points Okay, a little better, although I'm suspicious that you're not scoring yourself honestly, which is contrary to the spirit of the exciting young writers at 826.

7-9 points Come on! There's no way you did all that, even if you're one of the exciting young writers at 826.

10-11 points I'm just going to go talk with the exciting young writers at 826, because you clearly aren't taking this quiz seriously.

12 points Aha! *Aha!* You cheated! I knew it! You can't possibly score more than eleven points on this quiz! You are a scoundrel, and do not deserve one iota of respect from me!

With all due respect,

Lemony Snicket

Lemony Snicket *had an unusual education and a perplexing youth and now endures a despondent adulthood. His previous accounts and research have been collected and published as books, including those in* A Series of Unfortunate Events, 13 Words, *and his new four-volume series,* All the Wrong Questions.

This is the first time I've written an introduction, and I think it's the last. I choose to introduce 2003's writing for the *Quarterly* because that's the year I was born. At first I didn't want to do it, but then my tutor who helps me at 826 every day explained it to me. If you're ever asked to do something, never say no unless it's something weird. These stories are creative and amazing. One day you'll be writing introductions for my stories and someone will be writing about your story, and someone else will be writing introductions for that person's story, and so you get the point. So here are some wonderful stories from 2003. ✸

—SOFIA MARQUEZ, AGE 10, FEBRUARY 2013

2003

Volume 1

The President Needs $14 Trillion —and Fast!

MARNIE HATCH'S CLASS * *grade 10*
Thurgood Marshall High School

Three to four mornings a week, teachers bring their classes on field trips to 826 Valencia to experience two hours of high-energy collaborative writing. Students begin writing a story together, or in this case a play, and then, at a cliffhanger, finish their endings individually and each leave with a book of their own. Here we'll let you choose your own ending for the play.

* * *

FADE IN (INTERIOR CLASSROOM, DAYTIME).
[The class is quietly working on its assignments. **Callie** is busy searching the Internet for hot photos of Allen Iverson. Suddenly she gets an instant message. "You've got mail!" it says.]

[Message on screen]
You know who this is.

Callie: AHHHHH! Who the heck is that?

Dee Dee: Why're you screaming, girl?

Duane: [Rushes over to **Callie**. **Duane** is a heroic figure, stylish and charming. He smells of expensive cologne.]
I know who it is! It's George W. Bush!

[The rest of the class gathers around, curious to know what's going on.]

Marquez: He must need our help again!

[On screen]
Attention, class! I need you to raise money for your country! We need a gigantic bake sale! A bake sale to end all bake sales! We need to raise $14 trillion! And by this Sunday! Get cookin'!

Class: Oh my GOD!!!

Carlos: Mr. President, you must be trippin'.

CUT. FADE TO BLACK.

FADE IN (EXTERIOR AMUSEMENT PARK, DAYTIME).
[The class has spread out. Part of the class is at an amusement park. Another group is selling cookies at the stadium.]

Gordon: [Carries a gigantic box of cookies.]
Cookies here! Get your cookies! Please, people, we're trying to raise $14 trillion! By God, buy a cookie!

Larry: [By the entrance, playing guitar. He is waiting for donations. A small crowd has gathered around.]
Pleeease! Buy some cookies, man! I'll keep singing until we raise that money! I'll sing out of tune if you don't give me money soon!

Bonnie: [Running around, giving out pamphlets. An **Unidentified Person** comes up behind her, steals her box of cookies, and runs away. **Bonnie** and **Larry** wonder if they should chase after the criminal.]

Larry: Stop, you cookie stealer!

CUT TO (INTERIOR CLASSROOM, NIGHT).
[Everyone is sitting around, tense. They're worried because they've raised only $234.00. They have $13,999,999,886.00 to go. There's a crackle through the speaker. It's the president's voice.]

Voice Through Speaker: Where's my money, people? It's been two days and you're not even close!

Marquez: Mr. President, you're STILL trippin'! We can't raise that much money by tomorrow.

Voice Through Speaker: It's a matter of national security! The entire world is counting on your class to come up with the cash!

Ms. Hatch: [Bursts into the classroom.]
Hey everyone! I just won $90 million in the lottery! Can you believe it?

Gordon: Jackpot!

Carlos: Only $90 million?

Duane: [Still smelling great. He leaps to his feet.]
I have an idea!

Scraggly, Gray-Carpeted Suburban House

Notes from an Upcoming Novel

PHOEBE S. MORGAN ✻ *age 12*
Horace Mann Middle School

Phoebe Morgan was the first young author published by 826 Valencia; her debut collection, Starzen's Booty and Other Stories, *is in its sixth printing. The following are character sketches and a sample chapter.*

✻ ✻ ✻

I. THE JOHNSON FAMILY

Peter Johnson: The father of the family, a football-watching, bird-house-building, red-plaid-shirt-wearing, thirty-six-year-old, patriotic door-to-door vacuum cleaner salesman. He is the reason the family has moved from its beige-painted, scraggly-gray-carpeted suburban house, which lay in an anonymous suburb in Orange County. Well, it's more his job that made the family move to Sirkensville. You see, Tornado Machinery, the company that assembles the vacuums that Peter sells, decided to move its headquarters from Orange County to Sirkensville.

They did this because Tornado Machinery sales in Sirkensville were so low that in the last ten years only two items had been sold. Tornado Machinery was so desperate for sales to go up in the Sirkensville area that, being a fairly wealthy corporation, it opened a new headquarters in Sirkensville, hoping it would enhance sales. The new headquarters had an extremely small staff. Peter, being quite dedicated to his job, decided to transfer headquarters and move to Sirkensville.

Linda Johnson: The family's mother. Her occupation: homemaker. Skills: cooking, cleaning, and needlework. She was involved in a sewing circle back home in Orange County, along with other housewives and grandmas, these being her only friends other than a few soccer moms and old high school friends. But beyond these dull traits lies the key to the family's abnormality. She has been diagnosed with sporadic histrionia, a mental disorder in which one has sudden outbursts of fear and anxiety.

David Johnson: He is the ideal nine-year-old boy. He is kind, yet not exceptionally sweet. Smart, yet not ingenious. He has many friends, yet is not popular. He is true to himself, yet not so much as to become a deranged outcast. He adores sports, specifically baseball. He played third base while living in Orange County. He played on the school baseball team, the West Orange County Wolverines. His favorite National League baseball team is the L.A. Dodgers. He dreams of becoming a member of that team when he grows up. He loves the sport so much that he practices it whenever he has free time.

Sarah Johnson: She is basically the female version of David. She's a straight-A student, loves Barbie dolls and practically everything pink (though this does not include shaven rats). She engages in the most unimaginative little girly games imaginable, including House, Barbie (of course), Mommy, and Nanny, which is the only one that Sarah and her friends actually invented. She dreams of becoming a professional ballerina, just as David dreams of becoming a professional baseball player. Until then she continues to live the most depressing life a seven-year-old girl could ever even think of. That is, until she moves to Sirkensville.

MARY JOHNSON: She is the baby of the family, only being nine months old. She never cries, mopes, whines, or even nags. She opposes everything infants actually have talent at. All she really does is sit in the corner of the room staring blankly, with the occasional smile, pacifier in hand.

II. THE TZU FAMILY

Daniel Tzu: Daniel is the father of the Tzu family. He is also a mailman. A mailman with a deep, heart-crushing, soul-torturing, needle-heeled-boot-stomping-your-bare-foot kind of secret. The secret won't be revealed in this segment. You'll just have to read the rest of the book, lazy eyes! Anyway, Daniel is extremely cynical and sarcastic, but not so much in a chic, cool manner; it's more of a bitter, rude manner. He hates silliness and his happy-go-lucky wife, Daphne, who he only really married to get his green card quicker. He is originally from Montreal, Canada. He moved to Pasadena at the age of twenty-two, way back in 1973, because of his great fascination with palm trees and the effects of swimming pool chlorine on a head of blond hair. There he met Daphne, a young psyched-out flower child, and her many spacey, deranged pals. After knowing each other for only a matter of weeks, Daniel and Daphne decided to get married. They lived together in a Pasadena apartment, along with many of Daphne's friends, for a couple long years, until Daniel and Daphne got kicked out of their four-room apartment, evidently for not paying the rent. They lived on the streets for about three months. After a while, things began to seem brighter. Daphne was earning a degree in (can you believe this?) substitute teaching at Pasadena City College while, being quite musically talented, working part-time for a program that gave private guitar, bass, and banjo lessons to adults and children alike. When the couple earned enough money to get off the streets, they decided they were sick and tired of living in apartment buildings, with their little privacy and claustrophobia-causing bathrooms. They decided they would settle down in the sweet, peaceful suburbia of Sirkensville.

Daphne Tzu: Daphne Tzu, of course, is no longer the psyched-out flower child she was in her early twenties. She transferred to Salton City College, north of Sirkensville, when they moved, in order to finish getting her degree in substitute teaching. Over the years she has begun to develop a great interest in the "new age" way of thinking. She changes her religion every other month or so and tries to use natural alternatives for products like aspirin, deodorant, and chocolate. For the past week she has been practicing Hinduism. She believes that as a Hindu, it is her role to change the names of the family pets to those of Hindu gods and frolic around the house in a sari.

Eli Tzu: Eli Tzu is not your average *Star Wars*–watching, backwards-baseball-cap-wearing thirteen-year-old boy. He is one of thirty members of the town's Organization of Bohemians & Beatniks. In fact, he is the youngest member. He is often either neglected or taken advantage of by the older members, usually the boss.

Grandpa Alain: The father of Daphne, Connie, and Luna. He dedicates his life to his ten specially bred dreadlocked sheep dogs. He used to make a profession of breeding dreadlocked sheep dogs along with his beloved wife, Teresa. He loved his dogs so much that he named his three daughters after the first three sheep dogs he owned. Poor Teresa passed away a year after they retired. He hung a framed photograph of her beside those of all the sheep dogs that have passed on, above his bed. He lives in Maine, on top of a hauntingly desolate hill, along with his ten specially bred dreadlocked sheep dogs.

The Organization of Bohemians & Beatniks: The Organization of Bohemians & Beatniks is a nonprofit organization of young pseudo-beatniks (none of whom lived in the 1950s) and struggling artists who drift around the town giving free performance-art shows and poetry readings to the public. The thing that's rather bizarre about the group is its way of getting people to join. They select a random person and bug him or her until that person chooses to join the organization. This is what they did to Eli.

A SAMPLE CHAPTER, IN PROGRESS

The family manages to pack up its last belongings. They are all packed tight in large brown boxes and devoured by bubble wrap.

The dog (Lucky) and the cat (Tabby) are respectfully put into their brand-new portable kennels, which Peter had recently bought at Pet Dream, a chain of pet stores that overcharges for cheap merchandise.

Peter and David go to the moving-truck rental and retrieve a truck to carry their belongings. When Peter begins driving the truck, David becomes overly excited, this being his first time riding in a moving truck. "Oh, David," Peter says, scruffling David's blond bowl haircut, "I'm glad you can be here with me, son."

When they arrive at the house, they find Linda and Sarah wrapping up Linda's good china and silverware in newspaper. "How was the ride, sweetie?" Linda asks Peter after kissing him on the cheek.

"Wow, it was really the greatest," David says.

Peter and David leave the room saying they would load up some boxes.

"Be careful," Linda replies.

They manage to get everything inside the moving vehicle, including the animals, while Linda locks Mary up in her car seat and gives her a pacifier. It seems the family is ready to hit the road when suddenly David wails, "Wait! I forgot something!" He climbs up the Astroturf-laden porch stairs and the tan-carpeted hallway stairs. When he returns he is holding his favorite baseball cap. He hops into the backseat of the family's red SUV.

"What took you so long, sweetie?" Linda asks.

"Good-bye, old house!" Sarah cries, vaguely expressing any sign of real emotion. After about thirty minutes of driving, they stop at a gas station with a Moon Rams Coffee House connected to it. While pumping gas, David orders a caffe latte to go.

At 9:43 exactly, the family reaches the big steel sign that says WELCOME TO SIRKENSVILLE in pink cursive. Below, it reads MOST PEACEFUL PLACE ON EARTH. Two tacky illustrations of daisies are displayed, along with a couple examples of unidentifiable graffiti. The sign's edges are rusty.

The Johnsons' new house isn't far from the welcome sign. They reach it in four minutes. After parking in their new driveway, they slowly and carefully unload five sleeping bags so as not to wake the children. Sarah's sleeping bag has a massive Barbie ballerina printed onto its horrific, pink polyester surface.

"The crickets sound nice tonight," Linda says to Peter.

"They do, but I bet our new home will be even better," Peter replies. That night the whole family sleeps together on the living room floor in their sleeping bags.

The next morning they decide that they would like to go out for breakfast at an all-American diner/breakfast place. Regardless of the fact that downtown Sirkensville is only seven short suburban blocks away from the Johnsons' house, and that their car is still cargo-full, the family decides to drive to town instead of walk. When they arrive in town, they discover that in all of downtown Sirkensville, there are only two restaurants that even vaguely qualify as restaurants. They are the Beret Café and Prince of Thai Noodle II, which has a sign that reads, in small print below the name, THAI/AMERICAN CUISINE. The Beret Café has a rather large storefront window that displays many works of contemporary art. While passing by the café, Peter and Mary cover David and Sarah's eyes, thinking the art would have a bad influence on the children.

They are definitely not eating there. The decision is obvious: they are going to eat at Prince of Thai Noodle II.

Inside the restaurant is one of those annoying doormats that rings like a doorbell when stepped upon. Decorating the walls are posters for films that must have come out more than thirty years ago, and a diverse collection of strung miniature flags. The restaurant is filled with the sound of techno music and the essence of sweet-and-sour pineapple soup. A waitress with stringy hair and giant 1970s granny glasses comes from the restaurant's kitchen. "How many?" she asks in a rather high-pitched tone. The family is in a slight state of shock. They have never seen anything like it.

"Um, um, four, or actually, five including our little baby, Mary," Peter stutters.

"Okay, come right this way," she cries, her voice ever so painful and piercing.

Linda hesitates to follow the rest of the clan. She stands in the doorway, gazing at its many flamboyant decorations. The doormat rings several times. Peter makes an arm movement symbolizing "tag along." She slowly moves toward the table that Peter and the kids are sitting at. The waitress runs back to the kitchen.

She returns with four pink menus they can plainly see were shaped from laminated construction paper. The front has a dull crown printed on its pulpy surface.

"Daddy, will you order for me?" Sarah asks.

"Of course, honey," Peter replies.

An utterly hideous waitress comes shuffling from the kitchen. She has magenta skin and bloodshot eyes with yellow whites opened to their full extent, blinking constantly. She also sports a gnarly, rusty-red unibrow that resembles the tail of a squirrel, broken in its center, making it into a wide V. Her hair is in a flattop with a long thin braid sticking out of the back of her head bleached the same shade of blonde as Andy Warhol's wig. She carries a tray of bright orange and green beverages to a table close to the table where the Johnsons are sitting. While doing this, she chews a humongous wad of purple bubble gum.

As she approaches this table she begins to blow a bubble. When the bubble reaches the size of her bulbous head, the colossal sphere of candy and oxygen escapes from the safety of her mouth, followed by a long string of saliva covered in minuscule bubbles, and lands on top of the table...

That's a Horse Book of a Different Color

CARMEN DEMARTIS ✴ *age 13*
Alice Fong Middle School

"Most eleven-to-fifteen-year-olds don't spend much time looking backwards. But everyone in February's Story of Me autobiography workshop was surprised by how much they ended up having to say," wrote Jason Roberts, leader of this workshop, which, like all our workshops, brought students interested in a particular topic together for a series of classes taught by a talented volunteer teacher with expertise in the area.

* * *

The classroom is dimly lit by the glow of cheap light bulbs. A smiling teacher called Ms. Kwaanasomething babbles like an idiot in terms I don't understand! Bins of plastic toys fill shelves and counters! I manage to hide behind my mother's legs before being bombarded by reassuring comments from my alien teacher. Brightly colored drawings of former students cover all of the wall space! I can't take it! I burst into tears. What are they doing to me! Then they make me sit on a scratchy rug for what seems to be hours. Again, they talk on and on in some weird code. I find myself being ushered down a noisy hallway into a cafeteria. What went wrong with my life? Where is my mom? Who are these people? Here it comes again. The teacher. Why can't I understand her? She is making all of these kwung-kwangzooy sounds. The memory fades away in a blur of crying as I reunite with my mom.

My great-grandmother and my great-grandfather fled from the war in Russia to find better fortune in Canada. With not much more than a suitcase full of clothing and a one-way ticket to Canada, they started a life-changing trip to a foreign country. They took a risky trip on a ship that would save their lives.

On the ship, my great-grandmother had a baby that was born into a family with a very interesting background. The baby that my great-grandmother bore was (obviously) destined to be my grandmother. My grandmother (Minette) moved to New Jersey hoping to find a new home. In New Jersey, my grandmother met a young man named Arthur. Arthur and Minette married and ended up having three children.

This generation consisted of two boys and one girl, one of whom was to be my mother (you can figure out who). After living in New Jersey for most of her life, Gail moved to San Francisco in search of a home in the heart of a busy city. She moved there to attend art school.

Her husband to be was not in the United States for his whole life. His name was Bruno. He grew up in Italy for a few years of his life. After his mother died, he and his dad went to New York seeking a better life.

He spent most of his life in New York until he moved to San Francisco, where he met a "crucial friend."

Gail acquired a boyfriend while studying art. He was also Bruno's best friend. Gail's boyfriend was a player. He had a number of girlfriends before her. After meeting Bruno, she began to like him more and more. Soon after, she dumped her boyfriend to go out with Bruno.

Gail and Bruno had been going out for a while when Gail decided she wanted to be a nurse. She dropped out of art school to go to college and nursing school. Bruno encouraged Gail to complete college and pursue her goal. After she completed nursing school, she became a psych nurse at UCSF. After holding the title of nurse for a while, she became pregnant.

That's where I come in. On December 9, 1989, I was born. I had to be born early because my mom had a sickness that happens mostly among young African-American teenagers. What are the odds of that? After living in two different houses, we settled into a house in Bernal Heights. While I was in preschool, my mom became pregnant again. Unfortunately, the pregnancy didn't work out.

From then on, life was like normal. I continued to attend preschool. My preschool days were golden. They flew past me before I could say my ABCs. On my first day of preschool, I remember being led into the yard outside to meet the other kids. Right as I walked in, I saw some kids playing train in a line. Right off the bat, a girl named Karina asked me if I wanted to play. I was genuinely surprised at the girl's kindness and thoughtfulness. What was she thinking!? You can't talk to strangers like that! During my preschool years I learned my ABCs, how to spell *doll, dog,* and *cat,* and how to socialize with others. I also learned to share and trust.

After a summer full of R&R, I was brought to something called a school. It was just an open house (nothing to worry about). We soon found out that our neighbor's kids and Karina were also doomed to accompany us.

This school wasn't just any school, it was Alice Fong Yu. A.F.Y. is a Chinese immersion school, the first of its kind in bilingual education. The first day of school was already known to be hard. Just imagine having your first class be entirely in Chinese, a language thought to be one of the hardest to learn.

The first day of school was madness. The teacher was babbling on and on in some weird language. All I could understand was my name. After the first week, the shock had left me. In its place was motivation. We got what seemed to be a lot of homework in kindergarten, carefully tracing strange characters and illustrating their somewhat meaningless meaning. After a month of grueling work had passed, I was becoming familiar with all of the five recesses and all of the free times. Simple sentences were soon to be mastered. So far I had made three friends: Kai, Danya, and Karina. Kai was into make-believing, Danya was into sports and outdoor activities, and Karina was into having a good laugh. Keeping up with three personalities wasn't only a good learning experience, it was hard.

In third grade, I started to break up with Karina. This was anything but intentional. I had been friends with Karina for most of my life. She had been nothing but nice to me. Why was this happening? She didn't have to move. Moving to Burlingame was a practical decision financial-wise, but with her school being in San Francisco, a move equaled a school change. Karina met me out of school a few times before we stopped seeing each other. I think it was mostly because of the school she was going to. It seemed like she started to have different interests. She was a different person.

By the time Karina had moved, I'd had my Chinese name for two years. The pinyin (or the sounds of the words translated into English) sounds like *ma ga men*. In Mandarin it would be *ma jia wen*. A fifth-grade Cantonese teacher came up with names for every child who'd ever attended school up until first grade. For a class assignment, we had to look up our name in a special dictionary. The only thing that I came up with was "horse book."

A name, or something that gives someone a glimpse at their whole life's history in a few words, is an important part of your identity. Does that mean this teacher identifies me as a book about horses? Being confused and a little bit discouraged, I looked at the positives. A horse is a swift animal that is beautiful, elegant, and powerful at the same time. And a book is a gold mine of ideas and knowledge. Nowadays, I am proud to bear such a beautiful name.

In fourth grade, homework was becoming more of a reality. For all those years, math was taught in Cantonese. At times, this became a difficulty. Questions arose about high school.

How would we understand the teacher? What do we call the bottom part of a fraction in English? Why is the sky blue? These questions would remain unanswered for a while.

The school seemed to have its own problems. In fourth grade, there was a shortage of Chinese teachers...In our class, we went through two teachers in the course of one grading period.

Fifth grade was a nightmare. We had a teacher who had the temper of a lit fuse. Five, four, three, two, one...you didn't do your homework! Go to the office! Five, four, three, two, one... you broke my ceramic pig! Go to the office! She was a good teacher, but she had...interesting teaching strategies. We also had a very nice English teacher named Deborah Sandweiss. Ms. Sandweiss was a kind and generous person. Being only twenty-three years of age and hot off the press, she was a forgiving and inexperienced teacher. It seemed like she had been my teacher from the time I first entered through the gates of preschool. I was used to being hassled by teachers and constantly criticized. She was the first teacher who had been nice to me.

My next obstacle was middle school. Sixth grade came and went. And seventh grade was soon to come. An elite staff of teachers was hired to feed on their new naïve prey, us.

Since we were untrained in the laws of gravity, PE homework put our minuscule muscles to the test, while a strict Cantonese/math teacher drilled us on equations, characters, and mental math. At the same time, our Mandarin teacher and language arts/science teacher overloaded our brains with unnecessary facts and conversations. This was the first month of school. I am still shocked at how hard middle school was compared to elementary. We had way more homework and we had at least one test every week! Fortunately, I have finally adapted to the extra periods and the shorter lunch break.

Right now, I am thirteen years old, my lucky number is two, and I have a sad GPA of 3.29. I have two cats and two parents. Also, two good friends and two favorite classes. Here are two rules to follow in life: 1. Always do unto others as you would have others do unto you. 2. Always be a first-rate version of yourself, instead of being a second-rate version of someone else.

Poems

MADELEINE CONANAN
Children's Day School

In one of our earliest collaborations with a school, students from Children's Day School visited 826 Valencia frequently over the year to work on their creative writing and produce two publications. The following poem is from Land of the Poems, *a collection of work by the fourth and fifth graders of Andre Perry's classes.*

* * *

DOG GONE

My dog is gone, long gone he's been gone for days, weeks, months, years. Just kidding, he's only been gone for a few minutes and he's in the backyard.

BORED

I came home bored today. I didn't have a fun-filled day. Nothing new happened today. It's just the same old boring stuff. When will things get interesting around here?

HEN

There once was a hen whose name was Lack'n'quack. Who had a brother, the famous Sir Quackalot. As you can tell they didn't quack, or did they? Just kidding, they bark or at least

Sir Quackalot does, but Lack'n'quack meows. Nothing ever happens to them so the end.

RUBBER BAND

There seems to be a new popular toy, the rubber band. Everywhere I go people are either buying or selling rubber bands, and rubber band prices have gone up to $10 a box. When will this catastrophe end?

Please Remember to Suck Off His Finger with a High-Powered Vacuum

(An Excerpt)

KEVIN FEENEY * *age 16*
St. Ignatious High

This intensive writing workshop was designed to bring aspiring writers to the next level. Taught by Dave Eggers and Vendela Vida, the class used extensive contemporary readings to inspire the students to expand the scope of their work. The following piece was a result of prompts from the work of George Saunders.

* * *

I reached into my pocket, not knowing what I would find, but hoping something would be there, something I could brandish atop a Trojan horse. All I found was a packet of matches. I'd been eating alone lately at this diner downtown, a place called the Aging Fisherman. They had a little stream running through the middle of the dining area, and they'd pretend to fish out your halibut or your salmon or your catfish. Anyway, the matches were from there, with a little icon of an old man sticking his hand into a river, reaching for, of all fish, a tuna. These will do, I thought.

In one fluid motion I lit all the matches. I threw them onto the perfect lawn. Then I dumped a can of gasoline from the trunk of my car onto the fire. I jumped back as everything went into flames.

I didn't scream when I did this. I didn't run away. I just watched the place burn, like I was five again, like I was camping with my father and two brothers, like we were sitting there waiting for marshmallows to brown.

The fire department came, but not in time to save anyone. The cops came, too. I told them I burned down the house. They arrested me right then and still felt the need to shove me against their vehicle, even though they knew, and I wasn't going anywhere.

The whole ordeal made the papers and turned into the kind of thing people forwarded in e-mails. Barry Phillips made a pamphlet, which he distributed around the neighborhood, about what happens when you can't contain your anger. There's a number on the back for his yoga classes, which he says lower your chances of becoming "a crazed maniac."

My attorney made me see a psychiatrist to see whether or not I was chronically "a crazed maniac." I didn't mind. It was nice to get out of the cell for a little while. In fact, I kind of liked talking to Doctor Phelps. She seemed like an excellent listener. I told her that: "You're an excellent listener." She just nodded and then continued to ask me about what I felt about my crime, my childhood, my relationships, and my demons.

Once, at the very end of our session, when she had started to flip through papers and scribble on a legal pad, I asked her a question that had always bothered me: "When do you think we'll get rid of gravity?" This question seemed to disturb her; she did not answer, but scribbled more on her legal pad. I continued: "Once we can do it, you know what I'm gonna do?

I'm gonna jump up, just keep going up, up, up until I can get a good view of the earth, and I'm gonna wait for someone to wonder where I am, why I'm not around, and only then will I come back down—you know, flip the gravity switch back okay— but before then, I'll just wait."

I chose this year because I was born in 2004, and I wanted to write about the 2004 section. I like the first story in this section because it is a poem, and it was a good piece. The author knows all the details that are on the hill (you'll see). I also liked the third one in this section because it is funny. 826 is a good place because you can write and read and people help you with your homework. ✤

—VANESSA PEREZ, AGE 8, FEBRUARY 2013

2004

Volumes 2 & 3

Hill

SIOBHAN WILLING ✶ *age 13*
Home-Schooled

This workshop studied poems by major poets in order to inspire students' writing. At its completion, the students published a collection of their work entitled A Poem Is Worth a Thousand Pictures. *The following comes from that collection.*

✶ ✶ ✶

A hill on a farm. No cows graze upon this hill.
Only a lone eagle soars above the green mound
of dirt and grass.

Everyone who passes this hill remembers
some small detail from their life
that they have been unknowingly longing to
remember.

The Feminist Queen

CARSON EVERETT ✷ *age 15*
Lowell High School

Some students have become lifelong 826ers by taking workshop after workshop or enrolling in After-School Tutoring on the day they turn six. Others have just set up camp at a computer in the writing lab, typing away furiously whenever they can. Carson Everett has been one such student, producing hundreds of stories and publishing dozens of chapbooks over the years.

✷ ✷ ✷

It was March in the year 1212. The year the feminist queen Zuruna reigned in Colunia, a small country, which was near Bulgaria. Zuruna, the queen, spent much of her time helping the peasants with shipbuilding, public speaking, and storytelling. The Colunians almost had a war with their fellow tribe the Trelgondites over a water and land dispute. It is unknown by history books, except one: *The Book of Enotra*. *The Book of Enotra* was a book that was possessed by the well-known family Van Dietrich. They lived in Naples, Italy, then took the book to Florence in 1712. At that time a volcano almost destroyed it, but the magic within the book protected it. An innkeeper took the book to a place called Sofia, which is in Bulgaria. Humans and *The Book of Enotra* kept the record of this almost-war.

There was a master of arms in Colunia named Salatar the Shorter. He was more impatient than Zuruna, the queen. He was just over three feet tall with blue eyes, blond hair, and tough muscles. Zuruna, the queen, was twenty-four and almost eight feet tall. She was very strong as well. With her husband Lutung, she had a son, Velit, who was seven. Velit worked hard in Salatar's shop. Velit was a crafty swordsman and loved to make mischief for the peasants. Salatar disliked it when Velit used his sword to scare others weaker than him, but in general he was a nice boy.

Zuruna was a great event coordinator in the square of the capital of Colunia, Ralit. Zuruna spoke about the truth of the war that may come in a week. "All Colunians should not doubt that the Trelgondites are trying to attempt a horrible sack of our town. I urge the town to not worry about our town's safety because we have a good master of arms: Salatar the Shorter."

Salatar the Shorter came up with his pudgy fingers and said, "I think we should declare war on the Trelgondites now."

The queen Zuruna said, "No, I don't think we should declare war on the Trelgondites."

The Book of Enotra recalls the argument between the master of arms and the queen.

Salatar the Shorter said, "War is inevitable, we should strike first."

Zuruna, the queen, said, "I will not declare war on our fellow countrymen."

The Book of Enotra describes a tense moment of anger as if lightning had struck. The tall queen gallantly left the square to shed her queenly attire. She put on a brown bloon, a white berger top, and a red topcoat. All watched her meditate as she levitated three feet. You could hear a *hummmm*. Her husband came in to introduce the dark Viceroy Boulickia of the Trelgondites. Zuruna smiled while meditating and said, "The war is only about how much water and land we have."

Boulickia stomped the shoes he was wearing on the ground and said, "I want enough water and land or I will declare war on you."

The scribe wrote down the words of Boulickia. Zuruna stopped smiling and said, "Why?"

Boulickia said, "I want a war."

The scribe wrote the words down. Zuruna left and went to the shipbuilding yards. The scribe came with her to write about the next moment of her day. The cold day began at 4:45 AM, as the mystical queen began shipbuilding. She was the only queen known to shipbuild. Many sailors were shocked that a woman had already built four ships before lunchtime. All of a sudden Zuruna's brother Albert, who was the king of the Trelgondites, came to see her at work and ask her a question.

Albert said, "Zuruna, do you think I might die at the hands of fat Boulickia, who wants to be king instead of me?"

Zuruna said, "No, I don't think you will die."

Albert smiled at her and said, "Thank you, but you realize Viceroy Boulickia wants me dead so he can steal more land and water from you."

Zuruna said, "Hmmmm."

Meanwhile in Boulickia's castle, Boulickia said to his assassin dog, "Have you assassinated Albert yet?"

The dog said, "No, I haven't."

Boulickia screamed, "How dare you make a fool of me! I will send my best assassins to kill young Albert."

Meanwhile, in the shipyards, Zuruna said to Albert, "Don't worry, I'll protect you."

Albert gave a sigh and said, "I'm sorry, sis, but he wants war and he's the bastard of Boulickia. Will you please help me be safe?"

Zuruna said, "Of course, sweet brother, I'll help you."

Meanwhile, the Viceroy Boulickia wanted to talk to the best assassins about Albert being still alive. Boulickia's anger had been rising ever since the dog had failed, so he stepped up his plan to assassinate Albert. The assassins came in. One was a rat, the other an owl, and then there was a cat that was foul. The viceroy laughed his head off and looked around at the expensive wallpaper and expensive paintings of his great ancestors. Boulickia smiled at the assassins and they immediately knew he wanted them to fly to Ralit and assassinate Albert. The owl's claw held on to the cat, and the cat's paws held on to the rat's tail. The owl was on a rooftop when a gust of wind blew and landed them in the cobble street. A black cloak concealed the assassins until they got to Zuruna's palace. Albert was sitting on a wicker chair out in plain view of some peasants. The assassins were looking happy when they saw their target. The owl had a poison that could burn through the metal of a castle door. The owl used his beak to throw the poison toward Albert. Suddenly, Zuruna levitated the poison above the cobble street and knew it was an attempt to overthrow her. Albert's innocent blue eyes looked at her and then at the ground and he began to shiver in fear. The rat, owl, and cat returned to Boulickia without an injured Albert. Boulickia threw a saucer with a teacup on it onto the ground. His anger made the owl swoop into the chimney, the cat went under the table, and the rat scurried to the hole in the wall where he lived.

Boulickia's anger was so great that his hair smoked when the messenger from Albert gave him notice that he could not become king. Boulickia's fat body fell into a long chair and the chair broke. The viceroy felt comfortable lying there throwing saucers and teacups around.

Boulickia then said, "As the viceroy, I have warlike responsibilities and I get to own the Trelgondites and that milquetoast King Albert won't be king any more."

In Ralit, Colunia, *The Book of Enotra* recalls that Zuruna took extra precautions to make sure King Albert was safe from the evil grip of Boulickia. The sea in the background seemed more peaceful than the bickering of Colunia. Zuruna smiled at Albert and got him aboard a warship that she had built and then, for precaution, she used her own luxury ship to draw fire. The owl had dropped the cat and the rat on the royal ship to assassinate poor Albert. The rat had seen the queen and she wrestled with the rat and threw it all the way to shore. The cat bit her leg and scratched her knee.

Zuruna said, *"Xelia, Fougure, Peccaloi!"* This meant "Get away, cat!"

The lightning from her power had flung the cat all the way to where it came from and shocked Boulickia's mansion with electricity. Boulickia saw all his paintings ruined and his favorite lounge chair destroyed. Boulickia was becoming crueler and used slaves to protect his house from any more damage. Even when the slaves were doing a good job, Boulickia whipped them. Boulickia knew that Albert was alive and wanted him dead more than ever. Zuruna levitated into his court, holding the rat assassin by the ear.

Zuruna said, *"Xelia, Fougure, Peccaloi,* I will stop your evil plans and daily beatings."

Boulickia spat in her face and said, "What in heaven's name is Xelia? Whatever!"

Zuruna demonstrated on his house and said, *"Xelia, Fougure, Peccaloi,"* and the mansion came apart right away.

Boulickia screamed, "Nooooo!"

Zuruna levitated out right away to her castle. The tired sailors came to her castle to show how much a pain in the butt Albert could be. The rat and the cat decided to attack Albert again. The breeze from the ocean hid the smell of poison from normal noses. The rat fired a poison arrow at Albert and it hit him. He cried out in pain. Zuruna's eyes turned red and she levitated to Boulickia's house. She turned into an owl to listen to Boulickia and his assassins talk about what they had done.

Boulickia said, "So what happened to poor Albert?"

The owl laughed and said, "He is diminished. I saw the rat kill him."

The rat's yellow teeth chattered, "I got King Albert, see, and I fired the poison arrow, see, I watched him die, see?"

Zuruna, in the form of a smaller owl, landed on the cauldron that was sitting over the fire. The assassin owl hooted and swooped over to the cauldron, slapping his wings at Zuruna. Zuruna showed him her red eyes and flew out of the chimney and gave the owl a curse, *"Flupinia, Elsficola, Una, Spillenia, Ooaf, Hool."* This gave the owl another beak and the rat laughed at him. Zuruna levitated into the royal house and turned back into herself.

Things seemed to be done with; however, the assassin animals still wanted to kill Albert, and Boulickia decided to allow them to keep trying.

Salatar the Shorter roared and said, "I want war on the Trelgondites."

Zuruna said, "Well you cannot have a war, but you can stop Boulickia."

Salatar said, "Okay, I will."

The Book of Enotra recalls that Salatar did an interesting thing to keep the war from starting. Salatar crossed the border by mule. Boulickia fired arrows at Salatar, and the arrows bounced off him and hit the assassin animals. The assassin animals flew into the cold, dark forest. Salatar got into the forest as well and tracked the owl, cat, and rat.

The owl hooted, "I have two beaks and I don't want to be near Boulickia."

The cat roared, "I don't want to be either."

The rat chattered his teeth and said, "I need to run, a falcon is after me."

The rat ran as fast as he could to a forest cliff where the falcon grabbed him. Zuruna felt the imminent stopping of Boulickia and teleported to the falcon. The falcon tried to peck at her when she got near him.

Zuruna said, *"Islu, Lutu."* This meant "Drop the rat."

The Falcon dropped the rat. The animals decided to imprison Boulickia in the Xelia realm. Salatar prepared a spell that could put Boulickia in prison. Boulickia ran after the animals that he considered to be traitors and fell into the mysterious Xelia realm.

Salatar said, *"Sue, Roiu, Ifc."* This imprisoned Boulickia.

When Salatar went home he was considered a hero.

Zuruna said, "Albert, you get to rule your kingdom of the Trelgondites happily."

Albert said, "Thanks, sis."

The Mountain Patch-Nose Snake

JAKE WATTERS ✷ *age 16*
Lowell High School

In this writing workshop, taught by Dave Eggers, the assignment was to write a "cover story"—one using the themes and basic architecture of a classic story. The hope was that students would learn about story structure—what makes a story work—by walking in the footsteps of masters. The following story was based on Edgar Allan Poe's "The Tell-Tale Heart."

* * *

Yeah, I was nervous. I was totally nervous. Pretty nervous, really nervous. But when I decided upon it there was nothing to be nervous about. But I still felt so bad. I didn't want to steal it, but it just happened. The idea didn't even cross my mind. But still it happened.

Why would I even want to steal from him? I loved that store and I loved those sandwiches. I was a regular. I had gone to that store every day for a year and bought the same sandwich. Every day I walked through the door and the electronic beep sounded, he greeted me with a "How's it going today, boss man?" and asked me if I wanted the usual. The usual was a turkey sandwich with avocado and canned jalapeños, but no mayo. I hated mayonnaise, still do. It's awful. It's like eating fat sucked out of someone, put into a jar, and then onto your sandwich. Every day I walked down the aisles of shelves stocked with canned anchovies, boxes of crackers, and bleach, to the back, where they kept the sodas. Every day I contemplated my choices. I decided which drink would go well with my sandwich that day. I'd buy my drink and my sandwich and leave the store.

But last week it happened a bit differently. I walked in like it was any other day and I ordered the usual. I walked down the aisle of bleach and anchovies and I thought long and hard about what I would get to drink.

"Do I want an iced tea to refresh me in this warm weather?" I thought to myself. "I want to get a Yoo-hoo, but it makes my mouth all mucusy. It's all a bit too filling with the sandwich. But then again, so are half the drinks in this fridge. I could get one of those energy drinks, but they taste like cough syrup. Or I could get cough syrup. Or maple syrup. The choices are endless."

I decided to get a Yoo-hoo, and I pulled one out of the fridge. By the time I got back to the front of the store, my sandwich was toasting in the oven. Toasting is the most crucial part of a good sandwich—besides the bread and the other things in the sandwich. So it's really more of a luxury than a must-have.

So that day last week, I decided to break routine. I decided I wanted a candy bar. I walked past the front counter and I grabbed a Skor bar and stuck it into my pocket, with the intent of paying for it later. I took a swig from my bottle of artificial chocolate drink and began walking toward the counter. The wrapper from the candy bar crinkled in my pocket with every other step I took. It sounded like a cross between static, a maraca, and a crumpled-up piece of paper. I wondered what the noise was and realized it was the candy bar inside my pocket. My sandwich was done. I paid for it and the drink at the counter. It cost $6.55 and I dumped the change I got back into the tip jar next to the register. I left the shop and walked back home.

That crinkling noise accompanied me on my journey home. I reached into my pocket to get my keys. Instead of my keys I found a rectangular cube-ish thing wrapped in plastic. I took it out of my pocket and looked at the Skor bar in my hand. "Why am I holding a candy bar?" I thought to myself. "Where could this have come from?" Then it hit me like a sack of heavyweight boxers, each wielding a sack of featherweight boxers: I had just stolen from the liquor store. I had stolen a candy bar from the liquor store. I didn't like the idea, but it was true.

"Would he notice the missing candy bar? It's only a candy bar," I thought to myself. "Would he suspect *me* if he did notice? He wouldn't suspect ME: I go there all the time. Or would he? He does call me 'boss man.' I've seen people steal from there before and he never caught them. They didn't try and return the things they stole, but still he didn't catch them. How would I even go about returning the candy bar? How would I tell him I accidentally stole a candy bar? Would he think less of me if I told him? If I told him, would he purposely make a worse sandwich the next time? Is that possible? It's possible, all he does is put Italian dressing on it. But it's still good. I bet there's some way he could make a bad sandwich. I could pretend it didn't happen. I could just discreetly put it back in the tray tomorrow when I go there for lunch. Yes. That's it. That IS it!"

I decided I would just put it back in the box and pretend it didn't happen. The wrapper crinkled when I opened my hand. Anyway, pretty soon I looked down at my hand and saw what appeared to be the empty wrapper of the candy bar. Had I eaten it? I had.

I had no other choice. I needed to pretend I had not eaten/stolen the candy bar. I was confident that I could pull it off. He could not have known what I had done. I was so confident that I put the receipt and the wrapper in the pocket of my pants the next day when I went back, just to prove that I was untouchable, like Sean Connery, in that movie, except I won't get mowed down in a hail of gunfire. I would simply walk in, pay for my sandwich and drink, tip him, and leave.

I went to the liquor/sandwich market the next day. I walked through the front door. I heard the same electronic beep and was greeted the same way I had always been. I ordered the usual and looked above the ovens that the sandwich guy uses to toast the sandwiches. But now all the sandwiches on the menu were twenty-five cents more expensive. Was the candy bar I stole the reason for this? It couldn't be, right? How could a one-dollar candy bar missing result in a twenty-five cent increase in sandwich prices?

I heard something that sounded like a cross between static, a maraca, and a crumpled-up piece of paper. "The raise in prices must have been from that candy bar I stole," I thought to myself. I looked to see what was creating the noise but could not find a source.

"What's up with the prices?" I inquired.

"Meat—up," the sandwich man replied, his words drowned out by the crinkling. "—had—rices for—ears,—it's time to—ange—em."

"What now?" I asked.

But the crinkling became louder and louder. I felt like I had to scream to drown out the crinkle. I pretended I could hear him and I tried to make conversation. This was around the time that some hiker got stuck under a boulder and sawed off his arm to escape. It was all over the news. I tried to hide my horrified reaction to the crinkling for a while. I joked that cutting off one's arm with a pocketknife isn't that bad as long as you see the great outdoors. I paced back and forth in front of the sneeze-guarded table that held all the sandwich parts. I spoke louder and louder to get rid of the crinkling in my ear. No matter how loud I spoke or how hard I stomped my foot into the ground as I paced, the crinkling got louder. I played with my keys in my pocket in an attempt to silence the noise with a soft jingle. I knew that he knew what I had done. The crinkling could only come from the wrapper in my pocket. And he knew I was horrified by the noise. He could hear the crinkling in my pocket. He knew I had stolen a candy bar but pretended he didn't. He talked normally and rang up my sandwich as he usually did but didn't accuse me, as if mocking me. I had to scream; it was the only way it would end. The crinkling got louder, so loud that every crinkle sounded like a mountain being broken in half.

"Villain!" I screamed at the man across the counter. "Hide it no more! I admit it! I stole the candy bar! In my pocket is the wrapper and the receipt from which that sweet was absent! It is the crinkling of that hideous wrapper!"

Untitled

RADFORD LEUNG ✲ *age 10*
Commodore Sloat Elementary School

In Making Poems: Responding to Poetic Voices, taught by Laurel Newby and Renata Ewing, students studied poems by major poets to inspire their own writing. At the end of this workshop, students published a collection of their work entitled A Poem Is Worth a Thousand Pictures.

✳ ✳ ✳

Under the leaves the croaking frog
flies to the moon and blows the fire.
Away against purple ships I saw from
the bus that light blue rainbow as the
girl wanders about in the window of
doom. She wanted to say, "Now it's time to say
what you wanted to say," but doom sighed
instead. She steps into the dark and
gazes at the moon as coins fall from
the sky.

Have you ever been at an 826 or visited an 826? Well, from my experience, I can tell you that 826 has helped me in many ways. I remember years ago, when I was little, I was starting to go to 826 Valencia during a time when I was going through a transition. When I started at 826, I was changing from being in a public school to a Catholic school. Everything at the time seemed challenging to me. My parents sought the help of 826 so I could get help on homework. They did not only help me on my homework, but they helped me express my creativity, imagination, and stories through the writing classes at 826. Please enjoy because they are amazing once you read them. ✽

—SABRINA YERENA, AGE 13, FEBRUARY 2013

2005

Volumes 4 & 5

Dust-Silk Pouch

SALLY MAO * *age 17*
Monta Vista High School

Students in this writing workshop, taught by Dave Eggers, first learned various methods of creating fictional characters. Second, students interviewed each other, looking for interesting traits. Last, they were given an image and told to place the characters they'd created in a far-flung place. The assignment, of which one product is below, made for richly detailed and wonderfully imagined fiction.

* * *

Up ahead, the road widens to reveal a slipshod blockade of cars, carts, and cargo. A yellow-curry smoke stews the engine of Mr. Kendall's van as he bites at the tail of jagged traffic. James, neck pressed against the seat, awakens from a sweaty dream to the grind of sound.

    He has just suffered the same nightmare again. It gallops with him wherever he goes. He sees its lean legs and mane, its relentless tawny hooves swerving outside car windows, airplane windows, and bedroom doors, and its acrid breath, a familiar stench, clogs his nostrils. The ride up the mountain has rattled his dreamscape like some monstrous cataclysm, magnifying his terror. This time the rodents had done it. They were wearing green uniforms, the whole lot of them. They swarmed;

they crawled; they carried nooses, plans, kerosene, and razor-tipped whips. They were out for blood.

James asks, "Dad, what's a Nazi?"

"Eh? Are we having this discussion again?"

"What's a Nazi? What's a gestapo? What are they?"

"A Nazi is a kind of monster," Mr. Kendall declares, "the kind that enslaves people and the kind that performs cruel experiments. A gestapo is their secret police."

"What kind of monsters are they? Are they some kind of furry creature? Rodents, maybe?"

"I wouldn't say that. But Nazis are less prevalent than they used to be."

"I just had a dream. It was the chipmunks...it was the rodents who made up the gestapo. They wanted blood, Dad! They wanted blood and they're right here in India. I'm not sure where, but I think they're further up ahead. I'm scared!"

Mr. Kendall laughs. "Well, son, who could really blame the rodents? The very term 'guinea pig' implies some sort of cruel and unusual experimentation. Yes, if rodents took over the world, they'd be out for blood."

His father's hands sweat on the wheel, "This may take longer than expected," he says. "The hospital is beyond this village. If I get this right, it'll probably be within the next two towns. I hope that's the one she's staying in. Otherwise, we're out of luck."

What they are waiting for James doesn't grasp. He fidgets, chews on imaginary gum, and plugs his ears. Before this trip, India was a haze of cast-bronze Hindu idols, boiled-blood sunrises, young girls in jeweled saris and deep crimson makeup, and all that kind of exotic drone that keeps a dish of samosas spicy. But like any vision, this one has been extinguished. India isn't carved out of ivory. India bakes and suffocates. India is dirty, damp, and cauldron-colored. India sticks to the inside of his skin.

Suddenly he looks up. "Dad, is there a fire over there?"

Mr. Kendall squints. A shift in the opaque reveals an entire mountain burning behind the yellow mantle.

"Looks like a real conflagration," Mr. Kendall says. "So that's what the commotion is all about. Guess we'll be here a while, until they clear it. That's if they can. Why don't you go fetch us some cold drinks?"

James opens the car door and inhales the smell of charred mountain. The unpaved street bulges with trucks, vendors, bleached billboards, and pools of reflective tar. He glances at a Pepsi sign and hand-gestures for two bottles. He pops one open and gulps it down. Almost warm, it fizzes.

Just as he starts back, he sees someone. A boy around his age, brick-skinned, two watery beetles for eyes, staring at him intensely. It isn't surprising. James is a Westerner, with sand-dune hair and pale eyes. He sticks out like a camel in a mangrove swamp.

The boy notices James staring back and quickly averts his eyes. Behind him, a voice calls out. It is the boy's little sister, teacup face framed with a tangled black braid. He carries a dust-silk pouch in her hands. With her mourning eyes, black and gray like a mockingbird's, she stares past James directly at the fire, as if in a delicate trance.

James recognizes her. This is the girl he had witnessed being burned by the gestapo in his dreams. His vision of infinite loss, of time and pain melded, the stalagmites in a human heart. His vision of mercy defeated. She had been burned like a sack of dry wood, a ritual mask, a ragged field of dandelions.

He motions toward her, letting out a sound. "Run," he hisses, "Run away! Please, don't let the fire get you!"

The girl stares at him, wide-eyed, and tugs the torn robe of her brother. She doesn't understand. Her brother shakes a fist at James, his beetle eyes bulbous with fury.

Suddenly, James feels ashamed. Someone he loves is lying in some ancient hospital in the middle of a sultry day in India, unconscious as a newborn shrimp, and probably plundered of her possessions, and the only thing he can do is recount silly childhood nightmares.

He runs back toward the car. He sees his father on his cell phone and slips inside.

"What took you so long?" Mr. Kendall asks.

"It was the vendor line."

"I got a call from the hospital she's staying in. She's frantic. Her injuries and exhaustion don't ensure her safe trip back."

"What's wrong?"

"Apparently, she knows one of the folks who lived up there in the mountains."

"Who?"

"She is familiar with a certain family up there. The news says that a few houses were badly burned. Not sure yet of casualties. But one of the families is a close friend of hers. Apparently, they have one son and two daughters."

James opens his mouth. "I saw them."

"What do you mean, you saw them?"

"I saw both sisters. One I saw just now. The other I saw getting burned. She died, Dad, she died!"

"Wait a minute—how could you have seen her getting burned?"

"I saw her, Dad, I saw her in my dream. She was the girl's twin."

"Don't tell me such things, son! Arson and death are never good things to joke about!"

James starts to cry. He remembers the girl's vacant face, her tongue that spoke a fragile Indian. He wants to see her again. He wants to explain himself. He wants to make sure she's okay.

"Sorry, Dad, I'll be right back!" James steps out of the van and runs toward the site where he spotted the girl. He runs past the vendors, a shop with cheap carved Buddhas, and the trees that obscure the burning village. He runs past the bleating drone of the traffic.

He sees the girl and her brother. James, panting, kneels down before them and stares up, wild-eyed. "You're...surviving," he says. The girl's expression, no longer in a stupor, suddenly is a somber smile. Somehow, she understands. She holds out her satin pouch and inside is a wooden frame, a crude photograph of herself and her sister. They are identical. They wear red satin saris.

He smiles and weeps. Her braid brushes the side of his cheek. Her eyes are watery, like wishing wells. Behind him, his father's car trails. Mr. Kendall rolls down the window and motions for James to come back inside. James slowly rises and waves good-bye. He wonders if the girl was only pretending to understand. He wonders whether she would cry.

"It's a little bit clearer down the road. The smog's descending," Mr. Kendall muses, "I wonder if we'll make it to the next town in time."

James presses his cheek to the window and watches the girl disappear behind the smoke. The unpaved road shines with tar and footprints.

Quarterback'n

VINCENT CHAO * *age 15*
MetWest High School

826 Valencia tutors worked with students at MetWest High School in Oakland for three years, helping them hone their writing skills. The following story is from their 2005 collaboration.

* * *

My first pass felt great. That was when I knew I was going to be a quarterback. I started playing in third grade, and from then on it was history. I used to play on the concrete at school, so when I fell it hurt. When I reached the fourth grade, I joined the football team. When I got to practice, I didn't know anyone. None of my friends wanted to join the team with me because they were too scared to get hurt. The first game we played, we won. It felt great; it was our first win. All of the other games we played, we lost, including the championship game, which I wanted to win.

When I reached the fifth grade, Lavante, Jerry, and Corey (a few of my friends) finally joined the team with me. The first day of practice was terrible because we did everything wrong. The first game we played, we were winning at the half, 7–0. When the second half started, we had the ball again. We ran the ball in a reverse play and we got a touchdown. We won that game, 14–0.

After all of the practice, it worked out really well.

That summer I broke my finger. I had to face it. I loved to play football, so after school, my friends and I walked up to the center for football practice. We ran some plays until our coach came into the huddle. He said that this play will always work on the opposite team, but first we had to try it. When we tried it, it worked really well. The next two games we played, we won easily. But when we had to play against Garfield, I was nervous because they had the same record as us, 3–0. The game was rough. It turned out to be 0–0 at the end of the first half. When the second half started, we had the ball and I threw it to Lavante on the other side of the field. After the play, we played the "jet blue," which was the play that our coach had taught us. I screamed "hike!" and threw the ball. It worked and we scored. I was so happy. I felt like I was going to punch somebody from the other team.

As soon as the other team got the ball back, they scored. It happened so fast I didn't even see it. It was second and five and all we needed was a first down. Time was running out. But when I threw it to Jerry he bobbled it, and while it was still in the air, the opposite team snatched it from Jerry and ran for a touchdown. It was over. But we won the next game we played. We went to the championship game, which sucked because I had been there before and lost. So when the big game came I had butterflies in my body.

When the game started, the first pass I threw was an interception, and in my head I was thinking, "Dang, they're good." The opposite team had the ball and they ran for a touchdown. Their running back was really fast, and we couldn't catch him. We finally got the ball back and after a few plays we turned the ball over again. When the first half was done, they were winning by a touchdown, 7–0. When the second half started, they had the ball but they didn't get a first down until the third down. Then they threw it and got to our goal line. During the next play they ran for a touchdown, and so it was 14–0. We had the ball and I threw it twice, but they were both incomplete passes to Lavante. When we ran it, they couldn't stop us. I threw it to Corey and got a first down, and when I gave the ball to Jerry to run, we got a touchdown. The opposite team had the ball and threw the ball far and the guy caught it and ran for a touchdown. The ball went to us again. Time was running out and I threw an interception. It was over. I was screaming and shouting in my head like the world was going to end. But we had to go get our participation trophy. When I got home I went to the shower and started yelling.

After that, I was still at school, playing football with my friends. It felt good to be playing football again. I didn't have to think about that game anymore.

The Fabulous, Stupendous, Spectacular, Absolutely Excellent Day

Every week of this workshop, six-to-nine-year-old readers ventured through a different storybook. These pieces were written after reading Alexander and the Terrible, Horrible, No Good, Very Bad Day *by Judith Viorst.*

* * *

ROISIN McLAUGHLIN ✽ *age 8*
Clarendon School

It was December 31 (my birthday) at 4:44 AM. My dog jumped onto my bed and woke me up. I went downstairs to the kitchen. I had my breakfast of OJ and pancakes. Then I jumped into the TV and woke up the cartoons. Then I jumped out. Then I found a giant trampoline. I jumped on it for three hours! Then I played with my dog. Then I went to my ice skating lessons. After that, I went to my favorite restaurant for lunch. Then the twelfth *A Series of Unfortunate Events* book came out. I read it for an hour. I finished it. Then I flew to Disneyland for the rest of the day. Then I flew home. At night, I turned invisible and went to Golden Gate Park.

JOELLE PARK ✶ *age 7*
Notre Dame des Victories

My puppy (that I don't have) will wake me up. I will have bacon and eggs for breakfast and the bacon won't even have that much fat on it! Then my cousins Sara and Jennie will come with us to Lake Tahoe, and there will be a big snowstorm so we will go tubing, skiing, and sledding. And we will get hot chili cheese fries and sandwiches for lunch! After that, we will go home and play video games. Then we will take a long, long sit in the Jacuzzi. Then we will torture my other cousin, Joey's, hair. All of us will give him pigtails, braids, French braids, girlie-colored hair spray, and a mohawk. Then we will go horseback riding in the snow for 12,345 hours! Then we will have a mozzarella-ball salad and a big pot of bean-and-beef stew for dinner.

SHANNON GARCIA ✶ *age 7*
Alvarado Elementary

My brother woke me up in the morning, and today I am going to play with my friend Arianna. We are going to the park to play on the slides and the swings. And for lunch, I am going to eat a turkey sandwich with mayo, but I don't know what Arianna is going to have. Then we are going to Chuck E. Cheese's.

The Traveler Who Came from "The Paris of the Orient"

Interview With Steven Han, Shanghai, China

YAN RAN TAO * *age 14*
Balboa High School

During the 2004–2005 school year, sophomores from Balboa High School and tutors from 826 Valencia teamed up to record, transcribe, and edit—sometimes translate—the tales of 106 people who came to San Francisco from another part of the world. The oral history below is from the complete collection, which was published as I Might Get Somewhere.

* * *

Steven Han likes to travel. He has traveled through almost all of Asia and the United States. Nobody helped him during his journey. He just worked hard and saved money for his dream.

—Y.R.T.

I come from Shanghai, the most prosperous city in China. People used to call it the "Paris of the Orient." There are a lot of people who like to go to Shanghai because they want to know the new China there.

Shanghai is a big city with 23 million people. The residents of the city are from different places in China. It is the epitome of the whole Chinese culture.

I grew up in Shanghai, and had a very good education there. Since 1980, China has had a big change. It opened its doors, and there were a lot more opportunities. Now I want to know my hometown more, and to see different parts of Shanghai, see the new buildings. I want to go back. Speaking of my hometown, I want to thank my mother, because she gave me life and she took care of me very carefully when I was a child. I got a very good education because of my parents' encouragement.

I came to the United States in 1980. People had more freedom at that time. In the sixties and seventies, China had a cultural revolution. It was called *Wen Hua Da Ge Ming* in Chinese. People lost a lot of freedom. They did not have the freedom of speech. But now it's changed a lot.

When I was very young, I dreamed of being on ships from all different countries. I wanted to clean ships so I could get to travel for free. So when I was a child, I stood at the front of the port—Waitan (which means the "Shanghai Bay")—and saw many different ships from many different countries. I thought it would be a good way for me to travel. This is how I came to America.

I want to tell you another story. When I was in Shanghai, a long time ago, I met a Japanese man. At that time, Chinese could not speak to Japanese, but the Japanese guy I met was very friendly. I said hello to him, and he took pictures for me and I gave him my address. This was in 1987. Then he went back to Japan. Many months later, I got my first letter from another country. He mailed the color pictures to me. He was eighty-six years old, and I still keep in touch with him. In 1998, I went to Tokyo. I called him and told him I was there. Then I saw him. He was ninety-seven years old. He is still alive now, and I want to tell you that friends make you happy and you should give your heart to your friends. This was what I learned from my journey.

I have had many experiences traveling around Asia, America, and other places. When you have a dream, you try to make your dream come true. How do you make it come true? Just do it. Dream it, do it, believe it. You smile, you give your heart to others, and others give their happiness to you.

Nobody helped me during my journey. I just worked hard and saved money for my dream, and just stayed with my friends in America. I did everything by myself. That way every day was the the first day, the best day, and the last day of my life. I think the hard times made me grow up, and the hard times made me learn a lot from people. So I am a student forever and everyone is my teacher.

It was no different when I left my country, because I traveled around the whole of China and so everywhere is my home. So I came to America and it became my home. I didn't have a language problem, so I could easily touch the culture of this land. I traveled around almost forty-seven states in America. I learned many different languages from people, from American Indians to others. Everyone was my language teacher. Every day was a school day. When I travel around, this is my journey.

I want to tell you about the story of my journey, back in 1995, when I traveled to Alabama. I wanted to take the bus. I was waiting for the bus to go to Montgomery. A very old guy saw me and asked me where I came from. I told him I came from China. Then he asked me which city I came from. When I said Shanghai, he was very surprised and got emotional. He asked me if I wanted to come to his home. I said okay, I have time, so I went to his home and he showed me pictures. In 1928, he came to China; he was an American soldier. And he fell in love with a Chinese singer, a very famous singer. They both fell in love, then three days later, the American army left Shanghai and went to the Philippines. So he had to leave her. He showed me many pictures from that time and told me his love story. I still keep in touch with him. He is ninety-three years old now.

I traveled all around the United States, so I saw that each state was different. For me, there were a few reasons for coming to California. The weather here is good and the Golden Gate Bridge is here. And there is more Asian culture here. Also, there are many different foods here. The weather is good and the people are friendly—I think it is the best state. It is very easy to open your heart to exchange cultures and it is easy to make friends. I like it here. This is the reason that I live in California.

I want to tell you the truth about my first week in America. I had many pen pals before I came to the United States. I told you before that I think everyone is my teacher. People gave me new ideas and information, so that changed me a lot. So I thank them. I came to Chicago and saw my friends there. I stayed at their wonderful house. The first week, we went to the downtown area and saw some famous places. I had a wonderful week and it helped me learn how to communicate with American people.

The most important thing I can tell you is to study, study, study. Every day is the first day and the best day and the last day of your life. Learn more from people. Try to smile at other people and show your heart to others. That way you can have a heart-to-heart exchange.

(Translated from Mandarin)

Eight Ways to Get an Amusement Park

DANIEL ILLIG * *age 9*
Clarendon Elementary

If writing is a workout, this workshop taught by Doug Favero and Maren Bean was the stretching and warm-up exercise. The students, ages seven to ten, did their writerly calisthenics by following simple cues and writing for a short period of time. One of the cues was "Eight Ways to Do Anything."

* * *

1. Begging
2. Putting lemon juice in your eye and crying
3. Taking your parents' credit card
4. Making them feel sorry for you
5. Saving money in a safe
6. Asking an amusement park owner if you can have it
7. Putting a lemonade stand up for moola
8. Showing slides of how sad you are without it, then show slides of yourself with it

Shaking Man

SACHIEL FREGRIC NUNAZ MICHAEL ROSEN ✶ *age 8*
Fairmount School

In the Writing About Art workshop, taught by Abigail Jacobs and Taylor Jacobson, students wrote about works of art from both formal and emotional perspectives. These poems are the result of an exercise in which the students wrote about a piece of art that they had seen, read, or heard. This poem was inspired by the statue Shaking Man *by Terry Allen, on display at the Metreon.*

* * *

This statue is hard cold.
It walks to five homes at the same time.
The statue looks at everybody really fast.
The statue feels lonely and it says to me,
"You are human."
I type what it says.
I say to it, "Are you a statue?"
He says, "Yes."
His legs are quick.
His arms are strong.
I say to myself, "He is a statue and I am a human and we are still talking."

I was born on July 24, 2006, and my best friend was born one day after. My sister tried to name me Jacob, but my mom wanted to name me Myles, so Jacob became my middle name. Sometimes I come to 826 Valencia just for homework, and sometimes I come here for no reason. Other people come for the exact same thing. One day there were only three people here, so I thought everyone else shrunk in a shrinking machine. My favorite movies are *Transformers* and *The Avengers*. You should check out *The Secret of Blockbuster Hits*. It's about how blockbusters are so famous. I really liked the part about *Spiderman 2*. ✽

—MYLES CRAWFORD, AGE 7, FEBRUARY 2013

2006

Volume 6

My Great Dinner Party

ELLIOT TAM * *age 9*
Alamo Elementary School

In this workshop for students ages eight to eleven, the authors got to plan an imaginary dinner party, deciding what exciting guests would be coming to dinner, planning the menus, writing fanciful invitations, and outlining the entertainment that would accompany the meal. No imaginary expense was spared to assure the special guests a memorable evening.

* * *

"Hooray! It's Halloween!" Everybody ran to the newest place in town, Vampire's Bloody Graduation. I invited them and it was my treat. If you were at the party you would have seen: Yoda, Mewtwo, and Pikachu. You would also have seen Link, Kirby, and Bugs Bunny entertaining. After everybody was there, we ate dinner. We had blood, blood, humans, and more blood.

After dinner, we had dessert. For dessert we had money. Some people were full so they just kept the $3,941,567,208. At the end of the party, we sang "Good Riddance" and walked home.

A Hat

SABINE DAHI * *age 8*
Clarendon Elementary

Poet-Free: Free the Poet in You! was an introduction to poetry taught by Michelle Ryan in the fall of 2005. Students learned about language, rhyme, metaphor, and other poetic tools. They also had the opportunity to free-write and share the results aloud with their classmates.

* * *

A hat fell off a cliff
it fell on a child's head
and fell off the child's head.

The Secret of Blockbuster Hits

GUILLERMO GONZALEZ ✶ *age 12*
Everett Middle School

The *Straight-Up News is the cornerstone project of 826 Valencia's Writers' Room at Everett Middle School. Since 2003, tutors have met with student journalists in the Writers' Room weekly to help them write investigative reports and feature articles to produce the bilingual English-Spanish newspaper. The following story is from a 2006 issue of the paper.*

✶ ✶ ✶

What makes a blockbuster? A blockbuster movie can contain comedy or romance—a lot of movies are based on these subjects! There can also be a lot of action in a blockbuster, such as fighting, helicopter-jumping, and other stuff like that. A blockbuster has to contain an introduction about what is happening in the character's life, like what they want or what they like to do. Some movies, like sequels, begin with a bang and then introduce new characters in addition to old ones.

After this, the conflict is introduced. There is often danger and suspense involved in the conflict, which leads to a point when the main character, or characters, reach a life-changing decision. An example of this is *Spiderman 2*. Just when Peter Parker has enough to worry about, they do something else to make him blow his top, like put him down or threaten his family. All hope seems to be lost and they believe they have won, but then he realizes, through his internal conflict (internal conflict is when a character has a struggle within himself, in his head, and has to make a decision), that if he does not make the right decision, everyone will be doomed. This is the part that leaves you hanging.

The next part is the climax. The climax is the part when the hero has found a way to defeat the monster in his head and will now try to defeat the villain, whoever it may be (it could be a dragon or an old friend). The point is, the hero will have to try, try, try!!! Only one character will succeed, and guess who it is? If you guessed "hero," you were right! People respect heroes because they think, "He's cool. He just saved the world."

Then comes the falling point. This is when the conflict is resolved, everything is finishing, and the credits come on.

Juliet Snowden, thirty-nine, is a screenwriter in Los Angeles who has written the blockbuster *The Boogeyman*. She says that you can't just sit down to write a blockbuster. "If Hollywood knew what made a blockbuster, somebody would be getting really rich," she says. "You can increase your chances by 'packaging' a movie, which means getting a well-known director and famous actors, but it's still not guaranteed. The public decides what a blockbuster is." She talked about how the blockbuster *The Terminator* came from a very small idea. The director just thought of a robot stepping out of a flame, and the rest of the movie followed.

Snowden says she's been writing since she was about the age of Everett Middle School students, but that writing is still very difficult. She is now working on the script for a remake of *The Birds,* Alfred Hitchcock's famous movie. "I think it will be a blockbuster, but I could be wrong!"

"I've found that the only way I can work is to work on something that's interesting to me," says Ms. Snowden, who works with her husband, who is also a screenwriter, "If we don't think it's cool, the people who watch it won't think it's cool, either!"

The Case of the Sparkly Pink Hello Kitty Pen

EMILY MAYER ✶ *age 13*
Lick-Wilmerding High School

In the workshop Says Who, students explored the powers of the narrator through individual writing and group improvisation exercises. First the students took a look at a few famous narrators to see how those narrators told their stories. The students then entered the scene of a crime, discovering that what actually happens takes on a life of its own with each witness's account.

✶ ✶ ✶

PART 1: MARGO

She told me it was her sparkly pink Hello Kitty pen. I disagreed. It was always hers, never mine, and her excuses that my property was rightfully hers had, over the past few months, grown a tad unbelievable. Sheryl had been my steadfast best friend from the moment we laid eyes on each other in Mrs. Loden's kindergarten classroom with the rainbow posters and all the dolls in the world for us to invent stories for. I was fascinated by her plastic heart-shaped sunglasses that gave you a twin when you looked at them from the front, while she was entranced by my purple Barbie shoelaces I just got for my fourth and a half birthday. That was the first trade of our friendship. And now they had gone way too far. You know that girl you hate to love? That was Sheryl to me. She always had to be in control. The princess. I, the carriage conductor. But now I was going to stand up to her. "You can't have it," I told her, my arms folded tightly across my chest. But sometimes people just won't give up. I was about to use my weak arms to pull it from her when Tommy, her baby brother, waddled in. And I, making sure it wasn't her mom or dad or someone who would catch my act of shame, thrust my hand into her pocket. The pen fell on the floor. And as in slow motion, Tommy grabbed it in his little tattle-tale fist and chewed it. Sheryl and I both instinctively made faces of disgust and walked out, in order to paint our nails with the Hello Kitty plastic pink polish that came with the pen.

PART 2: SHERYL

How could she possibly say no? Had she ever said no before? Had the letters *n* and *o* together ever left her lips and reached my ear before now? I don't think so. I have always been in control. She's always done what I've told her to do, no questions asked. It's not fair! The pink Hello Kitty pen called my name, spoke to me, I swear. And so I took it. Isn't that how it has always been? I just knew she wasn't using the pen the right way. It's such a pretty pen. So sparkly and pink. So I took it. At least I could use it and appreciate it right. But then she, my very best friend in the whole wide world, betrayed me, sticking her dirt-caked hands into my new jasmine princess jacket. She stole it and it's not fair. But at least she didn't get to touch it for too long. Tommy, my gross, cootie-catching baby brother, trundled in and, using his slimy grip, stuck it into his mouth and chewed on it. The marker was lost to the cootie king forever. I almost gasped with horror. I looked at Margo, and she looked at me. And I remembered her brand-new nail polish and smiled. And she, I guess, realized she'd been wrong and smiled back. With one last glance of disgust, we flounced our hair and turned away. Here we were, Sheryl, the princess, and her faithful servant Margo, making a comeback.

2007 was my favorite year of all, which was when I joined the 826 community. 826 Valencia is a great place to write, create books, do homework, and, most important, have fun. Before I went to 826 I was not very interested in writing, but that has all changed. I love writing and am an inspired writer. What I also love at 826 Valencia is that you can comment on movies and get into the *SF Chronicle*, which I had a lot of fun doing. 2007 was a great year for 826 too. Here are some examples from what you are about to read: "He replaced his leg with a mango and he fell and squashed the mango." And, "Nikola Tesla was very attractive to women." ✱

—SANTIAGO DELGADO, AGE 12, FEBRUARY 2013

2007

Volumes 7 & 8

Magnetism

JUSTINE DRENNAN * *age 17*
Crystal Springs Uplands School

Every summer, 826 offers a one-week intensive writing workshop to high school students. During our Young Authors' Workshop, which we used to call the Summer Writing Camp, students take classes with novelists, spoken-word artists, screenwriters, and poets and leave with a chapbook full of new work on Friday. This piece is from the fourth annual workshop.

* * *

"It turns out,"
our physics teacher tells us,
"that Nikola Tesla was very attractive to women."
This is a slight digression from our
study of electromagnetism—
we've been learning about attraction
between oppositely charged
particles, and the force of that attraction
over a distance, and Collin, who had
dropped down to a lower energy level,
has become excited again to hear about Tesla's
compulsive habits: cleaning his fork and knife
with a napkin before

every meal; his irrational repulsion to
pearl necklaces. But soon even
Tesla has lost his draw, and
minds are leaping
to lunch with the girl five seats away,
and the oranges the cafeteria staff
always forgets to provide.

Martin Luther King, Jr. Day

EVAN GREENWALD * *age 13*
St. Mark's School

The Valencia Bay-Farer, *826's only in-house newspaper written by and for students, allows journalists ages eight to fourteen to flex their skills. Students express themselves by writing news articles, opinion columns, entertainment reviews, sports, profile, and humor. The article below is from a 2007 issue of the paper.*

* * *

Where were you on Martin Luther King, Jr. Day? Were you at your house? Were you at someone else's house? (And what in God's name were you doing at someone else's house?) Were you watching TV? Well, while you were performing trivial activities, the Yerba Buena Center for the Arts showed the ninth annual "Bring in the Noise for Dr. King" poetry slam. Thirty-three young poets, all under age twenty, came onto the stage and told the audience what they thought and felt about the world today. They spoke about a range of topics from Dr. King himself to the Bill of Rights. ("Now go read the Bill of Rights, burn it, and write your own!") The night was ripe with fresh talent and artistry. Though many of these verses were strongly profane, they truthfully depicted the world as it is.

Slam poetry is a method of writing and performing that allows you to say how you really, truly feel about life. It's a full blast of speed and emotion. You may use powerful phrases like "Bush is a man who is in control with a great wave of righteousness!" Or you could go for a completely opposite idea. It all has to do with how you, the poet, see the world.

"Bring in the Noise for Dr. King" was established nine years ago by a company called Youth Speaks. Youth Speaks's goal is to raise the next generation of writers by placing and immersing them in a creative, poetic, and emotional environment. They're like 826 Valencia, but focus mainly on poetry and performance. The most important tool Youth Speaks gives their students is the spoken word. They try to obliterate both racial segregation and mental boundaries by introducing and promoting poetry in these young minds.

When these young writers finish their poems, they are only halfway there. Remember, the program is called Youth Speaks. The kids then practice on the stage, giving their poems a kind of hip-hop-ish style.

Youth Speaks has been at work for ten years and is standing very, very tall.

I conclude this article with a question (don't worry, it's rhetorical): Where will you be next MLK Day?

Alcatraz

DAISY GUZMAN * *age 11*
Horace Mann Middle School

The following piece came out of a writing prompt during After-School Tutoring.

* * *

It's scary to live on an island surrounded by water.
Ghosts haunt the island and the people who visit.
The ghosts are old and rusty.
And so are the ancient bars on the cells.
The island is like the jungle with no place to escape.
You are trapped by cold water and sinking sand.
You're stuck, hungry, and worried.
There is no place to go and there will never be.

Maccanik's Adventures

ANTHONY HERNANDEZ * *age 10*
Paul Revere School

For six weeks every summer, 826 Valencia and Mission Learning Center, a literacy nonprofit down the street, have hosted a six-week camp for elementary school students. In Exploring Words Summer Camp, which we used to call the Summer Series for English Language Learners, students read, write, perform plays, create experiments, and practice literacy skills during their months away from school. This story is from the final chapbook of student work.

* * *

Maccanik is lost. He has a friend named Cooconut. He is on an island called Where I Am. He got lost because he was a stunt man and instead of landing in the desert he landed in Where I Am. He replaced his leg with a banana, but it was too short. Then he replaced his leg with a coconut, but it was too short. He met his friend Cooconut. He drew a smiley face on Cooconut, then he replaced his leg with a mango, but he fell and squashed the mango.

Then he was mad and tried to beat up a tree and coconuts fell. He tried to find Cooconut but a coconut fell on his head.

It only hurt for five minutes, then he found an airplane (that still worked), but he took it apart.

Bullet Points

SIMONE CREW ✽ *age 16*
Lick-Wilmerding High School

During the fifth annual Summer Writing Camp, thirty high school students worked with professional writers, poets, spoken-word artists, and tutors on expanding their repertoire of writing skills. At the end of the intensive week of writing, camp participants presented their best work to the 826 Quarterly. *This was one of them.*

✽ ✽ ✽

My life began when I tried your cereal.
    Soggy in murky-milk, dried fruit like drowning insects:
    Raisin Bran looks like dirt.
    But I trust you.
    The following series goes in a similar pattern; the lingering scent of Old Spice a constant trend—my accounts involve an establishing "us"…various encounters with sunshine-hollow memories like lifesavers;
    I never liked how there was nothing in the middle.
    Colorful but without calories to provide sustenance.
    This time thread of old novels smelling musty and comforting links my events…and a callus begins to appear on the second knuckle of the middle finger of my right hand; where pens are pressed hard because I never learned how to hold

my pencil properly and I am passionate. Paper cuts and blood down shower drain as I learn to shave: bony ankles making this seemingly simple task a health hazard. I am still skinny—and make up for said lack of bulk with big books and heavy vowel sounds.

The sticky feel of peanut butter cements my tongue to roof of mouth at lunch.

Best friend can make this really annoying noise that makes her sound like a sea lion/dying horse. I am jealous and subsequently spend years trying to re-create the eerie effect.

I never succeed.

I am trusted...or at least expected to be trustworthy.

The scent of clean laundry; pleasant but ominous in its need to be folded. My callus has grown.

On BART, I meet Mac. In his twenties he smells of alcohol. I ask him not to touch me and he obeys...

Aligning his defined jaw to mine as though sizing up my face to see if our noses match up like he wants them to.

He blows beer into my eyes as he says he is looking for friends. He claims

not to care

but I think

he cares too much—

because who looks for friends on the Daly City train at six.

I start to take care of people;

making a mantra out of Mac's stop so he does not forget... watching him cry as I leave the train. His tears forming the most recent

bullet.

Turtles Inside

ERICA KUNISAKI ✶ *age 13*
Hoover Middle School

Hoover Middle School students created literary works in which they expressed feelings and ideas through style and rhythm. In this workshop, which concluded with the publication of a collection, the poets worked within the realms of found poetry, free verse, and haiku.

✳ ✳ ✳

When you see "Turtles Inside" on a door leading
to a backyard, you may think, there are turtles in there
and since it's here in San Francisco,
yes, you want to see the turtles
but it's warning you not to go in.
You feel dreadful, for you want and don't want to go in.
It is the same feeling you feel when you want to
see what is inside a chocolate box and you feel temptation
to eat it
or a bag from Target that was hidden in a closet
and you found it and had the urge to peek.
Or maybe it was when you saw a Coke left on the dining
    room table.
You already had the feeling to have a bit of cream.
You felt the screams inside your head.
And you feel it now:
the door is whispering go in, go in.

Warm/Cold (The Sun, Orange Juice, Ice Chips)

MAYA GOLDBERG-SAFIR * *age 17*
College Prepartory High School

This piece also comes from the fifth annual Summer Writing Camp, in which thirty high school students worked with all kinds of professional writers and tutors on expanding their repertoire of writing skills.

* * *

HOW I REMEMBER I LOVE MY MOTHER:

My earliest memory is from my mother's arms, where everything is warm—her breath, my purple blanket, our hands together.

"Pick you up!" I'd insist, and she'd lift me into her lap. I don't remember her correcting me; in fact, as a child my words were rarely ever corrected. First there were the mispronunciations—for years I'd say "aminals" instead of "animals" and did not stop until one day in the car, my best friend Emma grabbed my arm.

"You're wrong!" she yelled. "Say animals!" I glared back, hurt and slightly stunned.

"Emma," I finally replied, "you lied about your dad being arrested by the po-lice, didn't you?"

"I did not!"

"It's the dumbest lie I ever heard!"

"You can't even say *a-ni-mals!*"

My mother eventually threatened to pull over.

And I never really learned how to spell. In first grade, I'd come home with stories about "liyons in afruka" and my mother would tack them to the wall next to my drawing of "graypes in froot bawls." When I asked my mother how to spell a word, she'd say, "Just sound it out, honey. That's good—"kay-ray-in." And that's exactly what I'd write down.

Later that year, Emma's dad died from a heart attack at the gym. Afterward, I would clasp my small hands to my mother's waist when she brought me to school, refusing to let go. In the early mornings, just before we left the house, my mother would hold my hair back while I gagged into the toilet.

Eventually, my mother made some decisions: I needed an ultrasound to find the cause of my vomiting and a therapist for my "separation anxiety."

"I am not pregnant and I am not crazy!" I screamed at my mother for a long time.

My father took me to see the doctor, where the gel was cold against my flat stomach and she assured us that my problem was emotional, not medical. I went with my mother to therapy, in a house near the border of Oakland and Berkeley—I looked for it recently, remembering the rose bushes in front, but stopped when I couldn't remember the rest—and I refused to speak for the first three sessions. I sat in silence on the couch, my face pressed into my mother's back until eventually I let my mother leave the room.

My therapist and I played pick-up sticks and walked down to the toy shop to buy dolls for her little house. We rarely talked about my fears. On the last day, we sat on the floor with my mother and ate Ben and Jerry's ice cream out of big containers.

I always insisted that therapy didn't help me, but afterward—though I still cried—I soon began going to sleepovers and new summer camps. I was probably wrong about therapy, but what's true is that by the time those sessions were over, I no longer loved my mother like I had in the years before. At that time, I was already hoping for a new mother—one with long dark hair like Audrey Hepburn or my sixth-grade math teacher, who was young and slender. By then my mother was far from flawless.

But in my earliest memory, I don't yet know any of this. I am in my mother's lap on the rocking chair and she has just finished singing "We Shall Overcome" in my ear. She rocks gently back and forth until I fall asleep, the blanket draped over both of us.

I like to think that in that silence, she held me so close, and I was so young that the connection between my mother and me was almost a tangible attachment. Sometimes I can still feel it, just barely, as I lay my head in my mother's lap at night when she is reading, when neither of us speaks and we are not angry. I close my eyes and think of her slow, deep singing, her fingers on my hair, and her arms where everything is warm. In these moments I am struck by how instinctual my love is, how she and I are, in fact, not that different.

LAST YEAR ON A SURVEY AT THE DOCTOR'S OFFICE I WROTE THAT I AM LONELY 33 PERCENT OF THE TIME, WHICH I THOUGHT WAS A LOT, BUT THEN I REMEMBERED:

I am nine years old, I have no friends, and I am happy. I decided that I have had enough of my third-grade clique, and I no longer sit with them at lunch. ("They're so impatient and bossy," I tell my mother. "And they always eat my food.")

Now I perch myself on the edge of the sandbox next to my assistant teacher Clarissa, who looks like a young, skinnier version of Frida Kahlo. She wears black sleeveless blouses with prints of large flowers and ties her hair in a thick braid or a messy bun on top of her head. I do not remember the sound of her voice. While I eat my bagel and cream cheese, Clarissa listens as I go on about my baby brother or how bad my dog Rosa smells or the time Ned Lutz threw a rock-filled balloon at my back and never apologized.

But one day she turns to me in the middle of a story.

"Maya," she says sternly, and I fall silent. (I hate when adults are angry with me, even annoyed or slightly impatient.) Already I am trying not to cry. Clarissa continues, "You cannot sit with me every day. I don't understand why you aren't playing with your classmates."

I feel betrayed and embarrassed. By the end of lunch, I stumble back to my friends, who are indifferent to my return, and eat the rest of my poppy seed bagel.

I now dread recess and lunch. "You're weird," Yalda and Rachel tell me as they share my leftovers. Why did you sit with Clarissa for so long?"

We begin to make tent forts out of cotton sheets at the corner of the playground. The sheets are musty and stained—our favorites have polka dots and scenes from *Winnie the Pooh*. We tie the ends to the fence in knots so tight we sometimes have to cut the sheets from their corners to get them off.

"No boys and no teachers allowed," we announce. I am told to stand guard.

Sometimes my friends conduct raids of the boys' fort, which is the play structure across the basketball court. I always stay inside, the blankets above just brushing my head as I sit on the cold cement and pick at pebbles, alone.

2008 was my first year at 826. It was difficult for me being new, but I made new friends quickly. We would go to the park and read great books. I loved the tutors. My favorite piece in this section is by Bo Yan Moran because she starts with a question and does a good job of answering it. I like that it encourages me to step outside of reality and use my imagination. ✽

—GUISEPPE PACHECO, AGE 11, FEBRUARY 2013

2008

Volume 9

Suit

CHARLIE GEBHARDT ✢ *age 15*
Oceana High School

Volume 9 of the 826 Quarterly *was dubbed the Apprentices Issue; as such, all of the pieces that follow in this section are from the Writing and Publishing Apprentices workshop. This workshop is a perennial favorite in which writers ages thirteen to eighteen come together to work with professional writers and editors on their projects.*

* * *

SUIT

All he ever wanted to do was go hunting with his coworkers, but bureaucracy had to complicate matters. He never had to deal with bureaucracy. His parents had taken care of such matters. Even when getting a driver's license, they had waited in line for him.

A sigh escaped his lips, the fourth of this week. Five sighs and suicide was justified, and bureaucracy, of all things, was driving him toward it. Bureaucracy. Bureaucrats had a tendency to send a person off to another bureaucrat to obtain some form or another. He was now outside the office of the vice president of oversight and gun control, most likely another tight-lipped, white-haired official. He pushed the door lightly, then harder. Was it locked?

He peeked inside and noticed a secretary slapping a pen across the surface of her desk. He motioned to her, trying to catch her eye. Exasperated, he threw his hands up in the air.

As he turned away, the handle caught his pocket, dragging the door with him. He entered the heavily air-conditioned room and strolled over to the secretary. He coughed once, twice.

"Um, excuse me?" he said.

"What?" she lisped, her tongue rasping against her neon-green retainer.

"Well I was—" he said.

"Here." She thrust a clipboard at him. "Fill it out. All blank spaces are required." Her eyes never left her pen as she twiddled it back and forth, back and forth.

"Could I have a pen?"

She looked up at him as if he was insane, as if she expected every man in a tie and suit to have a pen on hand, as if that was the norm. She reached into her pen cup and withdrew pen after pen, testing them. Each was more deformed than the next, some broken in half, ink dripping out. She withdrew a bitten blue one and ran it along the paper. A line of ink appeared along the page.

"This good enough for you?" she lisped condescendingly.

"Sure, thanks."

He walked over toward a scantly cushioned chair and took a seat. The clipboard was filled with the usual questions. Name, date, occupation, date of birth, social security number, mother's name and maiden name; he had memorized these long ago. He filled the paper with precise strokes and in the span of a few minutes he had finished. He walked over to the secretary and handed the clipboard to her.

She tapped the intercom button.

"Ms. Livingstein, a *man* is here to see you." She said *man* like she was spitting an unwanted gob of phlegm from her mouth. True, every day she only encountered men searching for a legal way to slaughter animals; they were sadistic brutes in her mind. She could only see him as one of *them*. She couldn't know that he was different.

She jerked her head at the door and continued to bounce her pen.

He took a deep breath, knowing that a bureaucrat never tolerated exasperation or impatience. He straightened his tie to the point of choking, gripped the handle, and pushed against the door. It didn't budge. He pulled and entered the immaculate room.

SYSTEM

"A *man* is here to see you."

Ms. Livingstein didn't know why she ever let herself succumb to having gun control added to her list of responsibilities. She thought it would sound good, would look good on her résumé, but she was mistaken. It had only led to headaches following visits from hillbilly farmhands who argued that they only wanted an M16 with antipersonnel rounds to keep away the "coons." The divorce with their wife or wives and their short-sighted anger had nothing to do with it.

Now this one had come. She could only hope he was at least well dressed. He entered the room, not slamming the door, not wearing overalls, and, most important, not chewing tobacco. No tar-colored spit would bubble on her desk after this meeting. He carefully sat down on the chair opposite her, not swinging his legs on top of her desk, not knocking over a prized family photo.

She was scowling in the photo in reaction to an overexposure of flashes and an overeager photographer. Her frown was out of place with the rows of easygoing smiles, smiles that conveyed endless patience. They had even been patient with her obsession with organization. As a kid she did not play with dolls; she organized everything, even her daddy's hidden magazines, which she had discovered during a cleaning raid.

He clasped his hands in his lap. A smile broadened across her face. He was dressed conservatively, his fashionable tie matching his sport coat. His head was resting on the tip of his index finger and thumb. His eyes gazed off into the corner of the room.

"Ahem."

"Oh, sorry. Bureaucracy is just getting me down."

An eleven-letter word! Grammar intact, she ran it through her head. It was music to her ears, and she smiled even though he was slandering the very system that she worked for, the very system that held her life together.

"I've just been trying to obtain a license for a gun to hunt for *such* a long time. Could I have paper"—he glanced down at his hand—"2AB34, concerning gun ownership and hunting?"

She opened a drawer, flipping through manila folders. She came to 2AB34 and froze. This man was just what she needed. He was a breath of fresh air. Why should she let him go? She flipped a bit further and pulled out another document. She didn't even have to look at it to know it was article 2AC34, but he wouldn't know the difference. She handed it to him along with her card.

"I hope this helps, but call if you need further assistance."

She flashed him a broad smile that he cautiously returned. And with a "thanks" he was gone. She congratulated herself. She had even given him her card. Then her euphoria disappeared. What if he didn't come back? Did she say something stupid? *If you need further assistance!* What a joke she was. She would be lucky if he ever came back. And she had broken a sacred rule of the office for only a *man*.

SUIT

"What an odd woman," he thought, "odd, but helpful. Oddly helpful, in fact." It was strangely out of place with the environment he was used to. Not that it was a bad thing. It was just so un-bureaucratic. He didn't know whether this was the end of it; in fact, he sincerely doubted it. He had too much faith in the bureaucratic system.

He threw the paper onto his cluttered passenger seat and floored his tinted-window Mercedes SLK, weaving in between cars in an attempt to reach his destination quicker, a destination he wasn't even certain about.

Home. Familiar, cluttered, everything a bureaucracy-filled day needs. A package lay on his doormat, a white return address stuck to the top. He picked it up and opened the door.

The air clogged the room. He walked over to a window, opened it, and stuck his head out. It was a beautiful day, its end signified by the sun departing. The last rays cast the clouds into majestic pinks, purples, and oranges. He could see the ocean glimmering as surfers waited for one last wave.

His life had always been just like waves, rising and falling. Now his life was centered on waves, stocks. They rose and fell, often bringing others down with it. It was a job. It was his life.

His coworkers often went out after work to a local bar called the Sunken Ship. True to its name, splinters stuck out of the bar and drinks akin to grog were served. He was never invited, though he wasn't even sure he could stomach a drink. He never was much of a drinker. Then he had been invited to hunt deer with them in two weeks' time. They had finally seen his greatness. But now ten days had passed and still he hadn't hunted at all.

He walked into the kitchen and set down the package. He opened the door to his refrigerator and pulled out a bottle of tequila. He poured it into a shot glass and gulped it down. A cry escaped his lips. It felt like the back of his throat had been branded with a hot iron. He pulled himself together and turned his attention to the package.

Now if only he had a knife to open it. "What could it be?" he wondered. He looked at the sticker; "Huntington International, Illinois." He settled on ripping the package open by hand, ruining its factory perfection. Layers and layers of stuffing later, he reached the end. A hunting knife set to his specifications. Its ivory handle was engraved with the words LIVE TO HUNT. This was the blade that would gut his first victim. He pulled it out of its sheath, admiring the glint of the blade. It slipped out of his fingers and nicked a patch of skin off his knuckle. The crimson blood and sunset slipped away. He gingerly put the knife back in its sheath and put it in his breast pocket.

He drifted over to his leather couch, faced out onto a full wall-length glass window. He set the glass down on an end table and grabbed the remote. Maybe it was time to go to the Sunken Ship.

SYSTEM

"Judy, dinner's ready!"

"Coming!"

Judy Livingstein rushed down the stairs, stopping just before the end.

"Casserole. Tuna casserole."

Her nose had been fine-tuned at an early age to detect the smell of tuna casserole, even blocks away from her home. Now she had to come up with an excuse before her mom suspected. It was easier to lie now that she was an adult. She could say she went out with friends for a late lunch. The reality was that she had no friends. All she had was her work.

"Judy!"

"Mom I, uh, I had a late lunch with friends from work." She started to head up the stairs.

"Look, Judy, you have to come up with a new excuse."

Judy stopped in her tracks. Her mom knew? She turned around and walked down the stairs.

"I figured one day you would mature and appreciate this. You like all my other cooking. You even like my stuffed cabbage. Where did I go wrong?"

Judy thought for a moment about being real. She hadn't been real with herself for thirty-six years. Thirty-six years with her mother. Where *had* she gone wrong?

"No, Mom, really, I did have a late lunch," and they both settled into their predetermined roles. She pretended to like her mother's cooking while her mother pretended to believe her.

Judy headed back up the stairs to finish *Mansfield Park* before her mom scolded her to go to sleep.

SUIT

His new clothes fit him perfectly. The tailors at Giorgio Armani knew what they were doing. He opened the door, his other hand tucked securely in his pocket. He shuffled over to the bartender, gathering stares as he went. He plopped down on the bar stool and rapped the counter.

"One drink, please," he said. He had practiced this phrase over and over before he went to bed last night.

The bartender turned his head, his voice laced with sarcasm. "Shaken or stirred?"

This comment unsettled him. He had no idea what it meant. Before he could guess, the bartender let out an uproarious laugh and turned around. The bartender's midnight skin contrasted with his white T-shirt. He held a cigarette between his thumb and middle finger, flicking the ash off onto the ground. He took a long drag off it.

"You're new, right? Of course." This brought another smile to his lips. "Let me guess, you're trying to prove you are one of the tip-top people."

"Did I ask for your opinion? Get me my drink!" he said.

"The problem is that you aren't one on the inside. You're like Jell-O in an earthquake. You quiver at the slightest trouble. You see, I know these things. Think about all the jobs in the world. Now think about the jobs that require conversation. A lot less, right? Yeah. So, those jobs, like taxicab drivers, hairdressers, and bartenders, such as myself, require us to talk to our customers. People come for the service and stay for the chat. I mean, really, a bartender can make the best drinks in town, but if he can't talk you through your problems he's out of a job. Every good bartender is a pseudo-psychiatrist. People expect bad drinks to gripe about and insightful comments to ponder. I mean look at women. When they have a problem, who do they want to talk to? Another woman! They want a shoulder to cry on and someone to sulk with. They turn to their mutts cuz they'll listen to them and won't say anything the women don't want to hear. Last are men cuz they'll want to solve the darn problem. People don't want to solve their problems; they only want to bask in their own negativity. It feels good to feel so bad. But, hold up, I'll make you a drink that'll settle just right with your mood. It's a specialty of mine."

He turned away, snatching bottles and vials right and left, throwing them into a cocktail shaker. He covered it, shaking it up and down with a force that could shake the needles off a porcupine. Blender to socket, a whirl of drink rising out of the cup. The bartender picked up the malt cup, pouring the grog into a chipper beer mug. A crack spiderwebbed its way from the top to bottom.

"Drink up. When you're done, we'll talk."

SYSTEM

The click of the intercom sounded. "Someone here to see you." By the tone of her secretary's voice Ms. Livingstein could tell this was an especially bad one.

A booming fist on her door. "Aight, y'all, I'm coming in." He burst through the door and stuck out his hand, his overalls gleaming in the rising sun. "Nice ta meetcha. I'm Charles," he bellowed, "Charles P. Fingerham, but you can call me Chuck. A pretty thing, aren't ya? What do they call you?"

"I'm Ms. Livingstein," she said. She had learned long ago that this flattery was to be ignored and was only used as a tactic toward getting their blasted gun, or guns, whatever the case may be. "So what can I do for you, Mr. Charles?"

"I told you, call me Chuck," he said.

"Chuck…"

"Well, I need some spare parts for my gun and I was out buyin' 'em when the cashier asked for some papers about me ownin' a gun and all. I never troubled with papers anyhow, never could read. I mean, reading never helped milk cattle or sow a field, and that's where Ma and Pa needed me most."

Her secretary was right, this one was bad.

"And, well, now I need to get my gun certified and whatnot. I want to, I really do, but they make it so hard. I mean they keep askin' for this paper," he glanced at his hand, "2AB34."

Her heart skipped a beat, and a nervous smile creased her face. This was the same paper *he* asked for. She had tried to put him out of her mind, but now here he was. A thought crossed her mind. She glanced at the hillbilly. Were they the same person, just in different attire? Was it all a joke? She looked hard at the hillbilly, but realized she couldn't remember *his* face.

"Well, do ya have it?" he asked.

"I should have it right here," she said, opening her drawer. She rifled through, trying to conjure his face. A minute went by and the hillbilly coughed. She looked up and noticed she had been running her hands through the stack from top to bottom repeatedly. She pulled out the form.

"Could you help me work through it, ma'm?"

"As much as I am able."

Several long minutes later of reading aloud and translating, the hillbilly was on his way and she was left alone with her thoughts.

Would he come back? Did he even care if he ever saw her again? He had said that he was depressed by bureaucracy, the very glue of her life. He hated bureaucracy! How dare he! And so she was left in an imaginary world where her ideal love tore apart her heart, leaving her with nothing.

SUIT

He was not used to puking. The awful taste coupled with the lingering effects of passing out gripped his stomach. He groaned, gripping the sides of the toilet bowl. He lurched up, his insides empty, empty of drink, of feeling, of soul. He stumbled back to the bar stool, grasping at it like a seaman in a hurricane. He pulled himself atop the bar stool, feeling his stomach gurgle in displeasure.

The bartender was dealing with other clients. That was good. He couldn't handle another story about the woes of the bartender's life. The bartender started to shuffle toward him. He put his head down, as if passed out, hoping the bartender would overlook him. The bartender grabbed a cocktail shaker and a few glasses and moved back to his clients. "That was a close one," he thought.

His shoulder was gripped by a hand. It tensed and released. He turned to the side and saw his coworker Peter.

"Oh, hey, Peter," he said.

"Hey, you've got something on your suit," Peter said.

"Oh, that's nothing," he said.

"I'm glad we ran into you. Well, um, we are going hunting at a country club that we're trying to get into, and, well, we need to look our best," Peter said, raising an eyebrow.

He understood what Peter was saying, that he would make them look bad, that he was not up to par, not elitist quality, that he was a nobody.

"Yeah, sure, I get it," he said.

"No hard feelings, right? Okay, we'll see you around," Peter said. Peter walked out the door with Joe following closely behind. "Did he buy it?"

"Yeah, he never doubted me for a second."

The bartender glanced at where he left his conflicted customer and saw only a pile of bills underneath a mug.

SYSTEM

Ms. Livingstein walked into the office, ready for work. Her secretary caught her sleeve as she walked past.

"Are you well, Ms. Livingstein?"

"Uh, yes, why do you ask?" Ms. Livingstein replied as she fussed with her hair.

"Well, you've been acting different ever since that *man* came in here. You know the one."

Ms. Livingstein knew; she hadn't stopped thinking about him since she had met him. As hard as she tried to suppress her feelings, they came back.

"Well..." Ms. Livingstein stammered.

"Just remember he's still a *man*," the secretary said, and settled down to rid her cup of all the broken pens.

SUIT

Tap, tap, tap, tap. The same old tap.

"You again?" the same old lisp.

"I got the wrong form." He held back the fact that it was her fault, that he had one more errand to run because she didn't give him the right form.

He took the outstretched clipboard again, sitting back down on the hard chair. He stared off into space, filling it out by memory. He had seen these types of forms so many times. He took a breath and sighed, his glazed-over eyes glimpsing a monotonous, secluded life ahead of him. He looked down at the clipboard and lifted up the paper. All he found was a new clipboard, not a single blemish. He looked up at the secretary; she was too engrossed in her pen to notice. He pulled a hunting knife from his inside pocket, opening it with a measured slowness. He pushed the point onto the clipboard, creating the first mark. Up, down, up, down, circle, down, down, semicircle, down, slant up, slant down: MARK.

It was legible, which was all that mattered. He walked up to the secretary, coughing to get her attention. She held out a hand, her eyes fixed on the computer screen.

"A *man* is here to see you," she shouted out to Ms. Livingstein.

He walked in, a glint in his eye. A glint he had lost for thirty-six years. She looked up outraged, then shy. He was not the glorified heartbreaker her mind had conjured.

"You gave me the wrong paper."

She looked up and then looked to the side. She bit her lip and looked back up.

"Can you give me the right one?"

She reached into her drawer, withdrawing a document without ever breaking eye contact.

He glanced over it. "Wrong one. Try again."

She reached back in and withdrew a different document. "Come on now. One more try."

This time she looked down and pulled out another document. She hesitantly moved it toward him. He snatched it from her, looking it over.

"Good."

He then proceeded to take the document and crumple it between his hands. He walked over to the trash can and opened his hand.

He looked her straight in the eye, his glint meeting her plead.

Her eyes stared vacantly at the empty chair. The door slammed shut and the tapping stopped. Moisture pricked the corners of her eyes and rolled down her face. Drops appeared on the desk, a desk unblemished before.

Is a Photograph Worth a Thousand Words?

BO YAN MORAN * *age 13*

The following essay was also composed in the Writing and Publishing Apprentices workshop in 2008.

* * *

I have heard the phrase "A picture is worth a thousand words" many times, but have stopped and taken it literally only twice. The first time was when I read it in a book. I thought, Could a picture really be worth a thousand words? Has it ever been proven? I decided to take on this mathematical and creative quest of challenging myself, to prove that a picture or photograph is meaningful to me in a thousand words.

My mother's interest in black-and-white photographs is very apparent around our house. There are, for example, three black-and-white abstract photographs on our living room wall. They have hung in those exact places for as long as I can remember, but I could not figure out what any of the images were for the longest time! Daily I would stare at them, but being stubborn, I never asked my parents.

Slowly, I realized that the photograph on the right is one of a dried, curled leaf, which looks to me like a sweatshirt with a hood suspended in midair. The one on the left, which I originally thought was an abstract sculpture, turned out to be a photograph of half of a female torso.

Although the sweatshirt and the torso are compelling, there is something about the middle photograph that has always captured my attention. It has a black, moonless, midnight countryside sky with darker shades of black surrounding it, like a dark Milky Way. Small, silvery puddles trickle down into a half moon, while two arms of silvery glimmers thrust out their hands and fingertips.

An accidental black spot, almost as if someone dripped some black paint off a paintbrush, causing dark lines to scatter in a pool of silver shimmering paint. Finally, a small pool of pure, silver unicorn blood has gathered from these trickles. The whole impact of the photograph, especially from a distance, is overwhelmingly mystifying.

As my daily viewings wore on, I pondered that it might symbolize good and evil by its use of contrasting black and white. But this conclusion was too abstract to satisfy my curiosity. I then started to surmise that the photograph had to be a picture of something on earth. At other times, I thought the photograph to be of nothing…nothing at all. The shapes and shades seemed to be so random that I did not think it could be anything real.

Three years and 1,095 daily viewings later, I suddenly realized the photograph was of a picture of a stream in the woods. From the stream, I could see the reflection of the trees around it, which I originally thought looked like the black Milky Way. The silver unicorn blood and the silvery arms, hands, and fingers were the stream. The huge black spot was a rock! The revelation completely astonished me. The mystery of the middle photograph was solved. I felt triumphant; however, this feeling was dampened by something heavy that gnawed at the bottom of my heart.

I am nostalgic for those times when I used to sit and stare at the photograph and let my mind run free. Frankly, it was more fun to let those wild thoughts course through my mind because I had the freedom to make the photograph whatever I wanted it to be. I was not restrained by facts. My mind made its own reality, and it was a reality I loved to explore.

It seems that these notions of reality and facts sometimes get in my way. They make me ask what I *should* be seeing. This photograph gave me a taste of what can happen when the apparent reality does not predetermine my thoughts. For example, sometimes I will say a piece looks like an octopus, but then someone who walks by may say derisively, "It's a flower. It doesn't even look a little bit like an octopus!" After someone says something like that, I look back at the piece of artwork and start to feel the almost gravitational pull of facts yanking me back down to earth, to reality.

Reality being a difficult thing to resist, I may even ridicule myself, asking why I couldn't figure out what the picture was. On those rare occasions when I do stand firm against reality's pull of facts, I find myself not concentrating on the photograph, but on pushing the facts out of my mind. The feeling was thrilling and much more satisfying when I was on the journey to figure out what the picture was, and the caption did not tell me what I was supposed to experience.

Whenever I pass the living room, I remember all the good times I had, just the photograph and me. This photograph taught me that being open, with no preconceptions, can be exhilarating. Even now, whenever I walk past that photograph, I do not automatically see it as it *should* be seen. I try to let my mind run free. This discovery, gained from a photograph, has not only found significance in my life, but the pilgrimage of this experience certainly has proved it is worth, at least, close to a thousand words to explain.

In a Delicate Hand

CHLOE VILLEGAS ✶ *age 15*

Writing and Publishing Apprentices is a workshop designed to guide all kinds of writing, which means that short fiction and essays are composed in the very same room as beautiful poems like this one.

✶ ✶ ✶

I have never understood birdwatchers,
or telescope keepers,
and least of all those who rise in the early hours
just to glimpse the melon-pink sun
before it takes on the brash yell of morning.

Why wait in such silence on a beautiful day,
simply to see an eggshell yield
some strange squawking fruit?

Why freeze in the cold of a windy hilltop,
your telescope toppling over in the wind,
simply to see a small reddish pinprick,
a cherry pit planet in the void of space?

If I were to quip about flowery plumage
or some celestial rarity amid the cosmos,
my private distractions would be quite acceptable.

But I will never be able to describe my findings.

And how is it that in a delicate hand
a thousand sapphire birds can take flight,
twirling on precious wings
through a gloriously infinite cosmos?

In 2009, I was about ten years old if I recall. I was a kid about four foot two and with a new hairstyle. Most of my childhood I always rocked a mushroom haircut, but this time I rebelled against my parents and decided to cut it off and have spiky hair. The year started with a memorable election that resulted in the first African-American to be elected president of the United States. The year before, the Programs Director of 826 Valencia, Jory, had come up with a brilliant idea. This idea was to write a letter to the president to congratulate him on his victory. One was my own letter, which explains what I wanted to happen in those times. 2009 was a good year: it started with good memories and finished with the best memorable experience. ✻

—MARCO PONCE, AGE 14, FEBRUARY 2013

2009

Volume 10

Cosmic List

KENNY DZIB * *age 8*
St. Charles School

Monday through Thursday after school, students fill the writing lab at 826 Valencia to work on homework with the one-on-one support of regular tutors. After they finish their assignments, students visit the Writing Table to respond to a prompt in their journals. The piece below was written during After-School Tutoring, though we can't take credit for any prompt that prompted such a list.

* * *

1. Alien energy adventure
2. Dark laser atomic
3. Mega lightning rush
4. Mega galaxy invasion
5. Dark assault clash
6. Solar cosmic shock
7. Cosmic clash adventure
8. Ultimate rustbucket rush
9. Iron rustbucket laser
10. Sonic spidermonkey fusion
11. Humongousaur rocket slam
12. Shadow quake doom

13. Iron rustbucket laser II
14. Lightning beam blaster
15. Ultra universe doom
16. Cosmic thunder clash
17. Robot shadow rescue
18. Sonic space spark
19. Turbo solar escape
20. Earth ambush invasion
21. Sonic hyper steel
22. Ultimate cosmic chase
23. Alien plumber patrol

Thanks & Have Fun Running the Country
Kids' Letters to President Obama

In January 2009, 826 National published Thanks and Have Fun Running the Country: Kids' Letters to President Obama. *The following letters are some highlights from the book, written by After-School Tutoring students, as well as some letters that weren't originally published.*

* * *

YOSELIN MARTINEZ ✶ *age 13*
St. James School

Dear President Barack Obama,

First of all, I am very happy you were elected president. When I was watching television on November 4, I started crying because I was so happy. Everyone in my neighborhood kept honking their car horns, yelling, and texting their friends about how you had been elected the 44th president. My friend's dad is going to open a new ice cream store right in front of my house, and they are trying to open it on January 20 in honor of you. My family and I have been talking about how, when you become president, it is going to be very hard for you because of the economy. Don't worry, you have me, my family, my friends, and St. James School to support you.

I have some questions and I would really love for you to answer them. Okay, here they go: How will you help all the United States immigrants? How will you help us students with our education? Will you try to make the United States a more environmental place? Well, those are my main questions. I just want to say that you are going to be a great president, and don't worry about anything, just remember that you have two wonderful daughters that love you and a wife that loves you too, and that she is as beautiful as a rose. I hope, Mr. President, that you don't make the same mistake as Mr. Bush about the war. If we want peace in our world we have to at least start somehow. We end up getting so mad about how we want peace in the world that we end up making hate.

My dream is to become a veterinarian or a zoologist because I love animals, and I think I would be more connected to our planet. I have dreams that I want to achieve; that is why my parents, my brother, and I immigrated here to the United States with our American Dream. My neighbors think that I am just another Latino who is going to ruin their lives. But they are so wrong. I want to graduate from college and show my mom that I worked my butt off. Well, thanks, and I hope you have a great time running the country.

Sincerely,
Yoselin Teresa Martinez Xonthe
(Peace in the world)

JONATHAN PINEDA ✶ *age 13*
Aptos Middle School

Dear President Obama,

I am thirteen years old, and I live in San Francisco. My parents were born in El Salvador. I go to Aptos Middle School and it's a good school. My favorite subject is science because you get to learn about life.

I'd like you to take care of your reputation, because gossip magazines are always trying to ruin a person's reputation. There's this magazine called the *National Enquirer* that's always making up gossip about famous people when it's not even true, just to make money. But sometimes that can fool people, so you should be careful.

I'd also like you to see what the people need, because if you do only what you want to do, that might not be what the people want. You should ask people to e-mail you what they think. Or they could write letters to you, like I'm doing right now.

I'd like you to accept immigrants as citizens. That way the economy would be better and there would be more workers.

Sincerely,
Jonathan Pineda

MARCO PONCE * *age 10*
Edison Charter Academy

Dear Mr. Obama,

Hi, my name is Marco, and I live in San Francisco. I am ten years old. I am writing this letter because I want to stop the war in Iraq and make the economy better. This is important because a lot of people are getting killed shooting at each other. Families are sad and worried about losing their loved ones; also, the war is very expensive. Mr. Obama, you should send the troops back to America. We can use the money saved to heal soldiers, and build schools for kids with low incomes and families with their needs. Thanks, Mr. Obama, for reading my letter about my problem. I like you being my president. I wish you good luck and to be elected again.

Sincerely,
Marco Ponce

DIANA PEREZ ✷ *age 10*
Edison Charter Academy

Dear President Obama,

Hi. I am Diana Perez. I am ten years old and I go to school at Edison Charter Academy in San Francisco. I bet your family is really happy that you won the election and so am I! I hope you visit 826 Valencia in San Francisco, so you could tell kids about your life. Also, I want you to visit my school in San Francisco. I hope you get elected again, four years from now.

Sincerely,
Diana Perez

I'm from Myself

ZOE KAMIL * *age 13*
Rooftop Alternative School

The following poem is from the workshop Teen Poetry: Love of Poetry Required. In this workshop, young poets learned new poetic forms, explored modern poets, and wrote new poems using the skills they'd gathered in class, performing them for friends and family at the end of the semester.

* * *

I'm from the brightly lit
hospital and forbidden
Chinese takeout.
I'm from bickering
grandparents and hide-and-seek
in the dark bathroom.
I'm from sandy preschool
boats, wishing for wet sand
to build structures.
I'm from ruby Dorothy
slippers and the Raven's house.
I'm from maniacal teachers
and times tables with all
the lights off.
I'm from men
with pink flamingo shirts
and stricter agendas
teaching me about tolerance.
I'm from losing friends,

from learning about what
I believe in.
I'm from whispers,
crying and not
getting invited.

When it was 2010, I learned how to do my multiplications. Then I saw more people come, and they needed help. But teachers never get tired and they never give up. In this section, somebody from James Lick Middle School wrote a poem about a pupusa. When I read it I was shocked because it was funny. ✻

—ERICKSON MARTINEZ, AGE 11, FEBRUARY 2013

2010

Volumes 11 & 12

Wednesday

GINA CARGAS * *age 17*
Lowell High School

This story is from the perennial Writing and Publishing Apprentices workshop, designed to guide whatever creative writing project students have in mind.

* * *

The mayor decided on a Wednesday to execute the elephants. He had never much liked Wednesdays, and this particular one had been extraordinarily frustrating. When he decided to execute the elephants, the mayor was sitting in the town's only laundromat—a place he hadn't visited in thirty years—wearing faded plaid boxers, a purple robe, and borrowed yellow socks. As he watched his clothes tumble in the washing machine, he ran a hand through his usually perfect hair. He squeezed his eyes shut in frustration at finding his hair in a disgraceful, wet disarray atop his head. He returned his hands to his lap and noticed that his palms were coated in an infuriatingly large amount of dirt. He twisted to scan the road outside the large window, praying no one was there to witness his humiliation. Luckily, Main Street was pleasantly devoid of the arugula-toting PETA members who had swarmed it earlier that day.

The mayor shifted his attention to the one person with a clear view of the mayor's embarrassing appearance. One of the Town Hall clerks fidgeted on the bench beside him, nervously eyeing the disgraced mayor without actually turning to look at him.

"Willie, I think I'm going to execute the elephants," the mayor said.

"Good idea," the clerk replied in what the mayor thought was an unnecessarily dull tone. The mayor watched the clerk expectantly, but his companion stared straight ahead. He was a young man who could have been the original inspiration for the phrase "tall, dark, and handsome," but the mayor found him to be somewhat lacking in the brains department.

The mayor wasn't sure it was a good idea. The local PETA members would be in a state of chaos—here he wondered how they could possibly intensify their disorder from the kumquat-flinging mob they had become that morning—while the circus owner had already threatened to sue. But the mayor was sick of the debate these elephants had caused, not to mention the torch-wielding protestors who had accosted him that morning, or the heap of legal paperwork awaiting him on his desk. The mayor should have been sitting comfortably in his plush office at Town Hall, but because of the elephants he was spending his Wednesday nearly naked in the laundromat with Willie Joseph, soaked to the bone with ice-cold water and covered in greens and eggshells.

The mayor wasn't even sure he had the authority to order the elephants' execution, but he was certain he could finagle his way into getting the city council's approval, even if he didn't get it until the horrendous beasts were dead. Well, if nothing else, he had Willie Joseph's approval.

He would have to execute the elephants tomorrow, before the crazy contortionists from the circus figured out what he was up to. Yes, that was perfect. He would march down to the circus tent and take the elephants into custody himself. A potential problem suddenly occurred to him. "Willie, how do you take elephants into custody?" he asked.

"I don't know, sir. I've never tried."

"Ah, well," the mayor sighed heavily. "I suppose I'll cross that bridge when I come to it."

"Yes, sir."

"I hate these fu-ferocious elephants, Willie," the mayor said, barely avoiding swearing.

"So do I, sir," the clerk responded. Perhaps he had been wrong, the mayor thought. The clerk really seemed to be a truly intelligent guy. He really knew his politics and gave such wonderful insight into the mayor's problems.

"It's their fault I'm in this d-darn tootin' hullabaloo of a fu-ferocious mess right now, Willie," the mayor went on. Swearing would have felt great, but the thought of the few coins in his swear jar at home stopped him.

"Well, technically, I think that's the PETA ladies' fault," Willie said slowly.

Despite the fact that they had pelted him with a bizarre mixture of produce, eggs, and high-heeled shoes that morning, the mayor didn't feel like blaming the PETA ladies right now. He couldn't kill PETA ladies. But elephants. Elephants he could kill.

"That's not true, Willie," the mayor said, easily passing over his companion's brief lapse in judgment. "It's the elephants' fault."

"Right you are, sir."

The mayor felt like swearing some more, but resisted. The last time he saw a man swear profusely, it was Bob Rutherson, right after the elephants stampeded his shed and trampled his award-winning vegetable garden, and Bob hadn't looked very dignified. Though he didn't look it now, the mayor knew that beneath his violet robe, he was a highly dignified man.

"I am a highly dignified man," the mayor declared for the simple reason that he liked the way it sounded.

"Yes, you are, sir," Willie said uncertainly.

"I will not be made a fool of, Willie."

At the look of confusion on Willie's face, the mayor felt a twinge of resentment. Even a man as insightful as Willie could grasp such a simple concept.

"But, sir," the clerk began, "you were made a fool of by those PETA ladies, weren't you? And the circus kids?"

The mayor had never really liked Willie Joseph, he suddenly realized. He was nearly as bad as those PETA radicals, the mayor decided. Yes, that was right. He had far too much to say. The mayor didn't approve of these rebel types, especially when they contradicted him.

"It wasn't the PETA ladies, Willie," the mayor growled. "And it wasn't those circus brats either. I'm telling you, it's the d—" he broke off and took a breath. "It's the elephants."

The mayor glared at the swirling, soapy water in the washing machine, willing it to hurry and cleanse the clothes within. At the jingling sound of the bells on the front door, the mayor swiveled to find the glass door swinging open. In a panic, he wildly attempted to flatten his hair as a lanky young man entered, struggling to keep control of the overflowing hamper in his hands. Dropping it on top of a washing machine with a thud, he nodded curtly at the mayor and Willie, then promptly turned away. The mayor continued to watch the young man with interest. He did not know this new arrival's name, but he was fairly certain the man was the son of Martha Puvinsky, the head of the local PETA branch that detested the mayor with such a fiery passion. My God, he hated those PETA ladies. The mayor had barely hinted at even touching the elephants and the "activists"—or so they called themselves—had immediately panicked, treating their own mayor like he was some atrocious specimen of mankind. It wasn't his fault, he assured himself. It was the elephants!

"Sir," Willie Joseph grunted, rudely interrupting the mayor's thoughts with that stupid rebellious voice of his. "The elephants didn't throw those eggs at you, did they?"

Fighting the urge to punch Willie, the mayor forced himself to give up arguing. Clearly Willie was too stubborn to ever give in to reasonable thought.

"No, Willie, that was the PETA ladies."

The young man had gone strangely still. The mayor sighed, aware that his words would certainly be carried back to Martha Puvinsky. Well, maybe she would at last understand that her whole misguided organization was being completely unreasonable.

"And the cream pies?" Willie pressed on. "And the water balloons? That wasn't the elephants."

The mayor squeezed his eyes shut and counted to ten, just as his mother had taught him.

"No, that was the circus brats. Kids of Twelve-Toed Thomas, I think."

Willie blinked at the mayor in apparent confusion.

"So it's not the elephants' faults?"

Their companion apparently could not contain a derisive snort. The mayor ignored it and took a deep, calming breath, another trick passed down from his mother.

"Not directly."

A long silence followed this statement, punctuated by the Puvinsky boy's rustling and the clinks of coins from across the room. The mayor tapped a beat on the floor with his fuzzy slippers, feeling his spirits rise. He was happy, and with good reason: He was going to execute the elephants tomorrow! Then this whole baffling legal mess would be over. He didn't understand the majority of it anyway—the permits and the insurance and the damage costs and Bob Rutherson's furious rants about his precious turnips—and he preferred the usually peaceful town to this controversy-filled, parsnip-flinging, mayor-abusing nightmare it had become for the week. All the mayor really knew was that the elephants were the reason he was sitting in a laundromat wearing his wife's robe and socks that had been left in one of the washing machines. They were the reason he was shivering from the chills as he struggled to both tolerate Willie Joseph and ignore Martha Puvinsky's son. The elephants had to be executed.

"Sir?" Willie said at last, and the mayor found he was no longer as irritated by the clerk.

"Yes, Willie?"

"I hope the eggs don't stain your clothes."

The mayor's eyes followed the suds swirling around the Puvinsky boy's clothes in the washing machine for a moment, contemplating the best way to kill an elephant. Would a simple bullet to the head do?

"Thanks, Willie."

2,000 Years in the Future

JULIAN KLEPPE * *age 8*
Starr King Elementary School

The article below is from a 2009 issue of the Valencia Bay-Farer, *826's only in-house newspaper written by and for students.*

* * *

Have you ever wondered about the future? What will the world be like in two thousand years? I don't know, but there are people who think about these things. I'm not one of them, which is why I called my friend Tracy Fieldestein. Tracy is a noted futurist. That is someone who writes and thinks about the future.

In the future there may just be one type of money in the world. Tracy said, "As long as there are people, there will be money." Just like Europe ended up using only one form of currency, we may end up having one monetary system. We may not end up using the euro two thousand years from now, but we will definitely have a singular world currency.

She asked me if it would be cool if there were solar-powered flying cars. My dad said, "Isn't it scary enough driving in San Francisco when the cars are on the ground?!" Tracy agreed: "People are lousy drivers."

Just as there will always be a traded currency, there will always be treasure. The question is, what will the treasure be? She told me how an original copy of *Superman* just sold for $400,000. You could have a gold bracelet with precious stones and it's worth $200,000, and a comic can be worth $400,000. Then Tracy asked, "What is treasure?"

The future may be scary and there may even be monsters. We may make monsters like in *Jurassic Park*. Maybe we can combine a chicken and a woolly mammoth, a chicken mammoth. "The human kind?" she asks. "Probably. There are always people doing monstrous things."

Do you know what is going to happen in the future? I don't, but ask someone else, maybe they know.

The Week of the Day

VERONICA SUAREZ-LOPEZ ✳ *age 10*
St. Charles School

The following saga comes from Look Closer/Mira de Cerca, *a chapbook published twice yearly in both English and Spanish that compiles the creative writing projects of the students in our After-School Tutoring Program.*

* * *

Once upon a time, there was a boy who loved his little dog, Prince. That boy was named David. First, when David's parents wanted to leave their house, David was just not in the mood. Second, today was the day to move. Third, after he was about to go into his room, it was perfect like a peach. Fourth, as soon as he was going to put everything in his room, he forgot all about his dog at his old house! He seemed so surprised that his parents never told him that they had given the dog away. Fifth, David always loved his Chihuahua. Sixth, David's parents had very sad news for him. Seventh, David asked what happened, and they said that his dog was very sick. And so David was about to cry like he never had before. Eighth, as soon as school was over, David just took off and went to the vet, and David went home and gave the dog some medicine. But David never told his parents that he had the dog. Ninth, after a couple of weeks, Prince got much better. But one night, it was David's first time sleeping over at his friend's house. A few years later David was in college and one day when it was his birthday his parents got him a dog. That was the happiest day of David's life. Then, when David grew up, David would tell everyone the story of how he grew up. But that wasn't it, because as soon as he was about to get married his wife was having a baby. David was so excited to have his first baby. And at the time, it was the baby's first year of Christmas when David had a second baby. David's life was getting better because all David wanted was a better life on Christmas Eve. He bought his little daughter a baby puppy, and his daughter was super happy and David gave her a big hug and a kiss. Years after, David was an old man and David's kids were growing up so fast. David got so sick; he was dying. Everything was swollen as a red balloon. On March 27, 2060, David died. All of his family remembers him in their hearts.

Shalhoubing

PAOLO YUMOL * *age 14*
Lick-Wilmerding High School

The following comes from the Writing and Publishing Apprentices workshop.

* * *

"Shalhoubing," he told me. "It's called Shalhoubing." Bobby Schmidt pressed his fingertips together, like the church minister.

Shalhoubing, as Bobby describes it, is the act of "becoming" the moderately famous Lebanese-American actor Tony Shalhoub. Tony Shalhoub has no idea that Shalhoubing is even being practiced.

"So are you impersonating Tony Shalhoub?" I asked him.

"God, no. It's not impersonating, it's becoming. It's like he's embodying us. Or, maybe, we're embodying him."

"And you just go out in the street, like what, like dressed up like him?"

"Me? No. Some of the other Shalhoubers do it. They say it 'enhances their experience.' But for me? No. God. This isn't marijuana, this is Shalhoubing." According to Bobby, there is a group of Shalhoubers who meet periodically, in taverns and cafés, or basements, to share their experiences.

"So what is this, really? Is Shalhoubing some sort of cleansing process?"

"No!" he said, offended. "No, not at all. If anything, Shalhoubing increases stress and mental instability." Then he licked his fingertip and decided he didn't like it. "One minute, you were barely something—this farmer, this factory worker, this schmuck—and then, the next minute, you're this famous actor. You've got responsibilities, pressure. Fear. Dignity. It's all very encompassing."

* * *

Two weeks ago, my girlfriend left me for this massive Spaniard. We were sitting out on the balcony, feet on the railing, when she turned to me and said, "I'm leaving you."

"For whom?" I asked intuitively, then: "How big is he?"

"He's more of a man than you ever will be."

An hour before, this had been the best day of my life. I realized this a few minutes after I stopped vomiting over the balcony. "Oh, man," I said. "Of course, there's this stupid food poisoning." She helped me clean myself up, kissed me on the cheek, and then left for the airport. She'd already packed her things.

I flew back and hid in my New York apartment the next week, in hopes that I could potentially be hiding there the rest of my life, with my limbs sprawled out on the futon, all so lanky and nonmuscular. I got called by my editor to do this story the same day I got back, and I sat on it for a few days. *This is it, huh,* I thought. This is me, this is me just writing stories about these other people. This is just what I do. I called back and agreed; maybe I'd give this one more shot. I hoped it would be worth it.

* * *

After the interview, Bobby took me outside for a walk around the town, an archaic patch of rural Tennessee. I honestly couldn't determine whether he'd started to Shalhoub. He was silent for a lot of the way.

"But you know, it's very exhausting, this Shalhoubing," he said as we walked past a drugstore.

"Then why do you do it?" I wanted to know. He halted.

"Well, why do any of us Shalhoubers do it? We do it in hopes that one day we won't have to be Shalhoubing. We'll just wake up one morning and we'll be him—this new person that actually isn't all that new. That is actually kind of familiar."

The Inside of My Mother's Life

AARYN BAKER ✳ *age 15*
Mission High School

Through the In-Schools Program, 826 Valencia tutors visit about fifteen different schools every year, working with students in the classroom on writing projects of the teacher's design. This oral history is from the project "Family Histories and Stories" with Ms. Riechel's ninth-grade Ethnic Studies class at Mission High School.

* * *

I interviewed my mother, who claims she's forty, but she's been forty for about three years now. My mother is African-American and Creole. I'm pretty sure she's a woman, based on the fact that she had a child. We live in an apartment complex in San Francisco. My mother goes to Heald College to be able to work at a hospital. She's like a big kid most of the time, but when she is serious it can come off as irritated. During this interview, she was wearing pajamas and this beat-up shirt my sister and I have begged her to throw away. It's her favorite shirt in the world, and it's older than she is. We did this interview in my room on the floor while watching our favorite

TV show, *Bones*. To explain her personality I'd say she's very moody, yet young at heart. She is highly professional.

What I learned from this interview about my mother that I didn't know before is that she had a rough childhood. She grew up in Chicago. It has a reputation for high crime rates. Back then in Chicago, you weren't allowed to be educated with other races. My mother claims she didn't see a white person until her mid-twenties. She had rags instead of riches. My mother says she didn't blossom until the summer before her senior year in college, so you can guess that her popularity level was low. She was raised by both her parents in one house, which you would think would be lucky. But for her, it wasn't. My grandmother and grandfather do not get along still to this day. When I imagine them, I feel bad for my mother. She had three brothers and a sister. One of my uncles passed away several years ago. We thought of him as holding the family together. "It made me stronger because it taught me to fight for what I want and need," is what my mother always says.

"One time there was a fire by your school and I was a worried parent and wanted to know if you were okay. The policewoman wouldn't allow me to retrieve you from the school because she thought I was lying about having a child that attended the school and accused me of being a drunk who was being nosy. She asked questions about me being intoxicated and if I ever abused drugs, and to me these assumptions were indeed because of my race. It wasn't until you came running down the hill as living proof that she allowed me to take my child home."

Doing this assignment, I not only learned how to interview properly, but I learned a lot more about my mother. Even though her concern can come off as annoying and overbearing, I have to recognize that she loves me and wants the best for me.

Outrage of the Pupusa

PABLO BARRERA ✶ *age 11*
James Lick Middle School

Since the 826 Valencia Writers' Room opened at James Lick Middle School in 2007, every student in the school has visited this mysterious room off the library to work with tutors on all kinds of writing assignments. Every fall, the entire sixth grade rallies to write and revise over two hundred poems in both English and Spanish with the aid of their tutors in the Writers' Room.

* * *

If I were a pupusa,
I would heat up with rage
in a hot, steaming frying pan,
knowing I would be eaten.
I'd later cool down
in my spicy salsa pool.
But my story ends here,
being chewed up into small pieces
because I am being digested
in a disgusting garbage stomach
by a man named Bill
who ate all of my brothers.

I like 826 because I have fun and get help from tutors. I have been published in "Look Closer," and my picture is up on the Young Writers' Wall. My favorite piece from this section was "I Used to Have a Dog." It's a whole story in two sentences. I liked this story because it's about a dog. I also liked it because it was short. It is hard to take care of a pet. I know because I had fish to take care of before. (No more fish to take care of now.) ✽

—EDUARDO DELGADO, AGE 11, FEBRUARY 2013

2011

Volumes 13 & 14

Letter to Malia and Sasha Obama

OCEANO PETTIFORD * *age 9*
Leonard Flynn Elementary School

After 826 students' book of letters to President Obama was featured everywhere from This American Life *to the* New York Times, *the elementary school attendees of the Exploring Words Summer Camp wrote a follow-up book to Michelle, Sasha, and Malia Obama called* I Live Real Close to Where You Used to Live.

* * *

Dear Malia and Sasha,

My name is Oceano. I am nine years old. My favorite colors are black and blue and purple. Can you cross your eyes? What's your favorite candy? What do you like to do when you are not studying? I like to draw, and I don't like to use colored pencils. If I went to the White House to visit you, I would like to play Little Big Planet and Ping-Pong. Is it weird being the daughters of the president? Does he take you out for doughnuts? What time is it in Washington D.C. right now? Do you wear fancy clothes? Can you speak any other languages apart from English? I know some words in Japanese. I live in San

Francisco. I like it because it is small. I used to live in Southern California. I love to play and I play a lot, and I love to write. Do you play any sports? I play Ping-Pong and go swimming.

Sincerely,
Oceano Pettiford

Considering Spies

EVA MELIN-GOMPPER ✶ *age 10*
Estes Academy

The article below is from a 2011 issue of The Valencia Bay-Farer, *826's only in-house newspaper written by and for students.*

✶ ✶ ✶

Spies are men or women who follow information, and walking humans that usually wear sunglasses, those I-know-you-but-you-don't-know-me looks on their faces, and disguises that blend in. There are maybe a hundred types of spies, so many I can't write about them all! I have never seen one, but I know someone who saw one or thought he saw one and that, in fact, was my dad. Spies (and secret agents) do not like to be seen, especially when they are on a case.

Here's the thing with culprits they spy on: The culprits they chase are usually thieves and the best way to catch a culprit is to set a trap. They make sure it is a sneaky trap so that the thieves basically catch themselves.

I think spying is what humans and nonhumans, like cats and wild dogs, like to do. I find it fun—not to be seen, but to see. I do not have a knack for spying. I like to crack nuts, which means to solve mysteries, and I used to be a spy in a way, but

I got tired of it. Spies have to be a little like superheroes, and I imagine it can become hard and dangerous. Then it stops being fun after a while. That's why I—or you—should consider being a spy BEFORE you become one.

For Girlz Who Have Considered Jumping Like Walking Is Too Much

LLUVIA QUINTERO * *age 13*
James Lick Middle School

For this project with Mr. D'Amico and Ms. Tyson's classes, eighth-grade students at James Lick Middle School worked with spoken-word poets from Youth Speaks and with tutors from 826 Valencia in the Writers' Room to write and perform their poetry.

* * *

When all I think about
are memories
that are too loud
all in my head
that I can't get out
lay in my bed
and I can't hear sound
all that's here is music
but it's not good
not at all
and I wanna fall
he sees me dance
he sees me prance
but I still jump
like walking is too much.

Escape

TIULI KULISHI * *age 14*
Gale Ranch Middle School

The story below is from the eighth annual Young Authors Workshop, a week-long intensive writing camp for high school students.

* * *

As a child, Reema had always been intrigued with the tiny detail that adorned her mother's wedding bangle. It was a delightful, ruby-eyed snake that was inscribed into the coral. Slowly, as the years passed, sindur (red wedding powder) filled the gaps, emphasizing its engravings even more. For hours, Reema would hold her mother's arm and twist the bangle over and over in her tiny brown hands.

Now, as Reema tied the twelve-kilogram weight to her ankle with a rope, oddly, she was thinking about this bangle. She brushed the tangled black hair from her weathered face. Although Reema was only nineteen, she was already a widow, a silent victim of a failed arranged marriage.

As she had sat in her room alone, night after night, she had cursed the Bengali customs of completely isolating widows, stripping away the nice things in life. She was confined to wearing only white saris, and forbidden to eat fish, which she had loved so much. Worst of all, she was expected to shave her head. She had refused to give in to this last tradition, and she now swiftly tied her long hair into a bun.

A silence had settled over her body, slowly and deliberately. It was too much for her to handle. The day her mother-in-law had knocked on her door with a pair of scissors to cut her hair, she knew what had to be done.

Strangely, as she readied herself to jump into the deep, dark pond that was surrounded by lush greenery, she felt no sadness or despair. She simply knew that this world had nothing left to offer her. And that was that.

Then, as if she were a lotus petal floating from its flower to be offered to the gods, she lowered herself into the cool pond and gave in to the weight that pushed her downward.

* * *

A small, grimy village boy is astonished as he witnesses a young white-clad girl give herself to the murky water. This astonishing scene causes the boy to yell, *"Dubaye gaache! Dubaye gaache!"* calling the villagers to help her out of the pond.

The next morning, as the hot sun lowered over Daspur, a tiny village in Bangladesh, the young widow woke from unconsciousness. She felt a sour punch in her stomach as she realized her failure, hearing her mother-in-law impatiently mutter, "How long is she going to sleep?" The air was heavy with perspiration and suffocating heat. Reema was too tired to open her eyes, for she knew her existence in the world was a matter of insignificance. She remembered the water and its embracing coolness, and as she felt beads of sweat form on her neck, resignation settled in. She dropped her head back into the pillow as she remembered how close she had been to escape, yet how far.

Not Your Regular Mermaid Article

AVA LYNCH ✳ *age 10*
St. Anne's School

The article below is from a 2011 issue of The Valencia Bay-Farer, *826's only in-house newspaper written by and for students.*

* * *

If you think this is one of those regular articles about mermaids, then you really shouldn't read this at all, because this is about different kinds of characteristics of mermaids and where those characteristics come from.

Some people may think mermaids are real, but other people (like my uncle) do not. If you believe in mermaids, you are probably wrong, because nobody has ever seen a mermaid, and nobody knows how mermaids give birth or what they eat.

Mermaids originally came from Greek mythology, but some stories may not be true. According to the *New World Encyclopedia,* some sailors may have confused mermaids with manatees because manatees hold their young the same way mermaids are said to hold their young. Also, sailors might have been confused by the way manatees' tails are shaped just like mermaids' tails.

In mythology, mermaids like music, and sometimes sailors were lured to their deaths by their beautiful voices. But mermaids may have been confused with sirens, even though sirens are half human, half bird instead of half human, half fish.

Well, you basically got all the facts out of me about mermaids. So I guess this is the end.

Girls

JUAN SALAZAR ROMERO ✳ *age 12*
James Lick Middle School

Ms. Hacker and Ms. Babcock's seventh-grade students work on many projects in the Writers' Room at James Lick Middle School. The goal for this particular project, called Snapshots, was economy with words. Students wrote creative short pieces using only the most essential words.

✳ ✳ ✳

I just want to write about girls.
I want to know more about them.
I'm curious about them.
I want to know what they like
so I can take them where they like.
But where would I take them?
We might go to a Giants game at AT&T Park.
We might go on vacation.
We could go to Brazil to the beach,
where the water is blue and the sand is brown.
We'd go swimming, and the fishes would be as bright as a piece of diamond.

I Used to Have a Dog

KAROLINA OCHOA ✶ *age 7*
Edison Charter Academy

This ominous piece was written in our After-School Tutoring Program during National Pet Writing Month, which we swear is a real thing.

* * *

I used to have a dog, and it is a hard job taking care of one. You have to feed it and take it for a walk. It used to be my responsibility.

DREAM: The DREAM Act

EMANUEL FLORES ✷ *age 13*
James Lick Middle School

Slick *is the cornerstone project of 826 Valencia's Writers' Room at James Lick Middle School. Started in 2010, the lifestyle magazine is produced twice yearly by eighth-grade journalists with support from tutors who help them interview, write, and edit their articles. The following story is from the Spring 2011 issue.*

* * *

Young children come to the United States at very young ages and grow up here as immigrants. The DREAM Act was created for these children. Children who weren't born in the United States risk getting deported back to their home countries where they didn't grow up. If they are lucky and do not get deported, they still struggle without many of the benefits United States citizens receive. The DREAM Act, which stands for Development, Relief, and Education for Alien Minors, is legislation that allows children who are undocumented to receive United States citizenship.

In order to receive United States citizenship through the DREAM Act, you must have arrived in the United States under the age of sixteen, graduated from an American high school or obtained a GED, and joined the United States military or gone to college for two years.

"The DREAM Act would affect our communities in different ways," said Carlos Sanchez, press advisor to Representative Nancy Pelosi. "The Hispanic community is affected. We're the community with the highest number of immigrants, and I think only positive things can come when you educate your own community." With the DREAM Act in effect, students would have the ability to make it to college and further in life.

A lot of people who are not immigrants may not care about the DREAM Act. They worry that there would be too many immigrants in this country if it passed. What is important to know, however, is that this law has really specific guidelines. "The DREAM Act is catered to students," Mr. Sanchez says. "It's been narrowly tailored so that only good things can come of it. The good things are that you have a more educated population; you have a whole class of citizens and of your community that is legal and is out of the shadows." This legislation may improve the United States because it will allow people who are educated to work in higher-paying jobs that other workers cannot do.

Many students at James Lick Middle School came here as immigrants at a young age with their parents. The DREAM Act could provide these students with a better life. Some students dream of going to college but worry that their immigration status might interfere. "It's catered to students who are trying to go on after high school to college and beyond," Sanchez said.

Unfortunately, the DREAM Act failed to pass the Senate by four votes. Obama, in his State of the Union address, pretty much declared that he would make it a priority to pass the DREAM Act.

If the DREAM Act does pass this year, it would really change America.

To Shakespeare or Not to Shakespeare

OLIVIA SCOTT * *age 13*
Everett Middle School

The following story is from the Fall 2011 issue of the Straight-Up News, *the bilingual English-Spanish newspaper produced by student journalists in the 826 Valencia Writers' Room at Everett Middle School.*

* * *

Friends, students, countrymen, lend me your ears. Shakespeare has been a popular writer for hundreds of years and now, after all this time, he can spread his writing to another school: Everett.

Shakespeare's birthday is unknown, but it is assumed to be April 23, 1564; he died fifty-two years later on the same day. He lived in Stratford-Upon-Avon, wrote approximately forty plays and 134 sonnets, and wrote all his plays for the acting group he was in. They were so good he even played for the queen, Queen Elizabeth I.

Shakespeare has been in your place many times before. It is thought that Shakespeare enjoyed education at King's New School. The conditions were hard, as they sat on wooden benches from 6 AM to 5 or 6 PM with only two short breaks. He shows this in *As You Like It,* with a boy "creeping like a snail unwillingly to school." He also made up many commonly used words like *bedroom, dawn, majestic, torture,* and *tranquil,* as well as having many influences on people and books alike. Did you know people have counted how many commas he wrote? It totaled 138,198. He also influenced many novelists, such as Herman Melville and Charles Dickens.

If it meant so much for these famous authors, wouldn't it be a good tool for middle school students? Mrs. McNally-Norman, teacher at Blackheath High School, thinks "children should start learning Shakespeare at an earlier age so as to get used to his language and so they do not despair when they are suddenly faced with a seemingly incomprehensible soup of Shakespearean English." As Mrs. McNally-Norman said, if children were taught Shakespeare earlier, their minds would adapt to the older language and comprehend more of his "soup," so they would enjoy the story rather than be too stressed to enjoy his writing. Katerina Edgar, a student at Blackheath High School, says, "I like how he uses metaphors, similes, and word order to give a piece of writing its richness. I also like the way he uses rhythm to give his verse another dimension."

Even if you taught Shakespeare in a modern context it would benefit the students, as they can emphasize and relate to the scenes in Shakespeare's plays. Not only that, but it can benefit their writing, as well as their use of the English language. Just as Isabella Scott said, "Shakespeare has made me the person I am today."

Electro's Diary Entry

DONTRELL HARDEN ✶ *age 10*
Junipero Serra Elementary School

The following flash fiction (no pun intended) was penned at our Exploring Words Summer Camp.

✷ ✷ ✷

Dear Diary,

As soon as I woke up, I felt something was wrong, so I shot a lightning bolt into the air from my mouth.

I remember when I came here to 826, it felt like a morning rush hour. I was the shy girl who sat in the corner. Soon I was at the Writing Table. I saw kids fill up their minds with imagination for the future. That future is giving our minds information and help to see that they may be helping future doctors, lawyers, and artists. So the Writing Table may be the hands and support for tomorrow. From Darkness being a character, to a Latina girl in the Mission, this year has it all. ✻

—JESSICA BERRIOS, AGE 9, FEBRUARY 2013

2012

Volumes 15 & 16

Conversations with Walmart Cat

LUCIE PEREIRA ✶ *age 15*
Gateway High School

The piece below is from the spring 2012 semester of the Writing and Publishing Apprentices workshop.

* * *

My cat Wally likes to sit on top of the television. When the TV is on, it warms his furry orange body until he overheats and his eyes roll back in his head a little bit, his pupils tiny slits of black in a yellow iris.

Sometimes his tail will hang in front of the screen, obstructing some crucial detail of whatever I'm watching. If characters stay in the wrong spot right behind the tail for too long, they become registered in my brain as having a fluffy orange face. Once the camera angle changes and the actor's true face is revealed, the character seems like a completely different person to me.

Annoying as it is, I leave Wally be. He's going through a rough time—he's getting to be an old man now, and all his friends have died. Last month I had to put Rufus, my other cat, to sleep when he got sick. I remember handing over his wiry gray body that stretched as I lifted it.

"Don't worry, he won't feel a thing," the doctor assured me, and I believed her. Rufus's blue eyes blinked drowsily with tired understanding.

When he was gone, I went home to deliver the news to Wally. He was confused at first about why his buddy hadn't come back with me. When the realization hit, he didn't take it very well. Then again, Wally doesn't take anything very well.

I adopted him as a birthday present for my wife around six years ago, back when we were first married and right out of college. He yowled so loudly during the car ride home that I lost it and pulled into the parking lot at Walmart.

"Shut up!" I shouted. "You unappreciative little furball! For a mangy cat picked up from a homeless shelter, you'd think you could be a little more grateful and shut your trap. I am about this close to dumping you in the Walmart parking lot and taking off."

He still didn't shut up. When I told my wife, Ellen, the story, she nicknamed him Walmart Cat, though his name had originally been Gary. Of course, he didn't take his name change very well. He hadn't taken his original name very well, either. But that was Wally.

Now he looks at me from his perch on the back of the sofa while I eat breakfast. He still seems depressed, though he'd never admit it.

"I'm sorry, man," I tell him. "I miss Rufus, too."

"Screw you," he replies with a hiss, not missing a beat.

"Believe me, I understand. The grieving process is difficult. I feel your pain. And, hey, if you ever need a shoulder to cry on..."

He eyes me for a second, then slides off the couch, landing on the carpet with more of a thud than he used to make. He saunters off and then returns a second later in Ellen's arms.

"Good morning," I greet her.

"Morning," she says, "The cat seems upset. Did you say something to him?"

"What!? Me? Never! I was completely sympathetic and caring and—"

"Don't bully him, Scott, he's sensitive. You know that," she chastises as she snatches her glasses from the kitchen counter. "I'm going out for brunch with Tracy, okay? Have you seen my car keys?"

"In your gray purse in the side pocket," I answer, shooting Wally a glare as he hops off of Ellen's shoulder and weaves his pudgy body between my legs with a smug expression.

"Thanks," Ellen calls over her shoulder. She's already almost out the door and on her way.

"What time will you be home?"

"Umm…twelveish, I think. Will you pick up something for dinner?"

"Sure thing. Have a good time."

"Thanks! Bye!"

And she's gone. Wally sneers as I pick up my cereal bowl and dump it in the sink.

"Lazy," he comments.

"Be quiet," I snap. "It's Saturday, for God's sake."

He rolls his eyes and settles down on the chair I just vacated, taking care to rub as many orange hairs into the seat as possible.

"I was sitting there," I mutter indignantly, but I know how to get him to move. I reach for the TV remote and the television flickers on. Wally jumps down immediately from the chair and races for the TV and nestles on top of it. I notice that he waddles as he runs. Stretching out, he begins to lick his coat clean.

"You're disgusting," I tell him. "You bathe yourself in your own saliva. Think about that."

"At least I bathe myself at all," he retorts.

"Very funny." I point a finger at him and plop down on the couch opposite from him, ignoring the reality show that lights up the TV and focusing on his grouchy orange face.

"You know, you're going to have to wash those dishes eventually," he lectures. "Ellen hates it when you leave your mess around."

"Everyone's a critic," I sigh, throwing my hands up with exasperation. "Seriously, who are you, my mother? And by the way, just because you're a grumpy old man doesn't mean you have to act like one all the time."

"I'm old, but I'm wise," he says slyly. "Which is more than I can say for some people."

"Okay, seriously." I switch off the TV and he meows loudly in protest.

"What'd you do that for?"

"I'm trying to get your attention, hairball. Is there something you'd like to talk to me about? Something we need to clear the air about? Anything at all?"

"No, no, and definitely not." His tail flicks with agitation.

"You sure about that?"

"Turn the TV on and maybe we can have a little chat," Wally tries to bargain.

"Deal."

I press the power button to appease him and he begins to purr with delight.

"Your turn."

Wally's yellow eyes dart toward me and I hold his gaze steadily. His body tenses. "You killed him," he spits suddenly.

"Whoa, whoa, whoa, slow down there. Let's get our pronouns straight. By 'him,' you mean Rufus?"

He doesn't answer. His eyes move back and forth across the room, debating. Freedom? Warm TV? The scales are about even.

"I didn't kill him," I say softly.

His eyes abruptly stop moving and he stares at me.

"Yes, you did," Wally states.

I shake my head. "No. I. Didn't."

He leaps off the TV and stalks away, fuming.

"Fine," I say loudly, "Be that way."

I pick up some novel that Ellen's been reading from the coffee table and flip through the pages for a while. I try to save her page, but I forget. Soon Wally comes waddling back through the living room toward his food bowl, not even bothering to grace me with a sideways glance.

"Ready to talk?" I ask him.

He eats for a bit, contemplating, before making his way over to where I'm sitting and plopping down in front of my feet.

"Talk," he commands, scowling.

"Rufus was sick," I explain. "You know that. He wasn't eating. Do you remember how bony and unhealthy he looked? He was already dying, slowly and painfully. I did what I had to do to end his suffering. You didn't want him to suffer, did you?"

I examine Wally's reaction. He closes his eyes slowly, then gets up, stretches, and ambles over into the kitchen. A few minutes later I hear awful, choking noises. *Is he dying?* I wonder with a momentary panic. That would be unexpected. Wally's too selfish to die just to stage a protest. He enjoys food and the warm TV too much to be a martyr. I rush over to the kitchen to find him hacking up a hairball onto the floor.

"I still hate you," he croaks.

I have to laugh. "Of course you do, Walmart Cat. And I hate you too."

Cuties with Prosthetics

CALISTA NICHOLSON ✳ *age 8*
Buena Vista School

The article below is from a 2012 issue of the Valencia Bay-Farer, *826's only in-house newspaper written by and for students.*

* * *

Once upon a time, there was a dolphin named Winter. She was three months old when a fisherman discovered her caught in a crab trap. The trap damaged her tail, so scientists took it off. Then they made a prosthetic tail for her. Not one prosthetic tail, but fifty prosthetic tails! And it took two to three days to make each of them!

The two scientists who made them all were (drum roll, please!) Kevin Carroll and Dan Strzempka. Kevin was driving home when he heard that a dolphin had been stuck in a crab trap. "Oh no!" he might have thought, because he called the Clearwater Marine Aquarium and offered to help. He helped because his mom was always caring for people, and he's helped animals and people all his life.

"I grew up and volunteered at a hospital for children. Whenever I would come across a little bird or an animal that had been injured, I would make a splint for them," said Kevin Carroll. They're two really cool scientists, and they're my favorite.

But Winter isn't the only adorable, beautiful animal that has a prosthetic something.

There is a kangaroo named Stumpy. They found her, and she had lost her leg. The procedure to give her a new one took an hour and a half. According to a Time.com article, "The Wild World of Animal Prostheses," the prosthesis was made out of carbon fiber, which can spring back to its original shape.

Next up, there is a *cuuutiee* dog named Sally. She was found in the desert of Kuwait with three legs and a bloody stump. It took four hours to rescue her. Scientist Erick Egger, a small-animal orthopedic surgeon at Colorado State University, made the foot for Sally, and then he actually adopted her!

Second to last, there is an elephant named Chhouk. He was found in the forests of Cambodia, and his foot was badly infected. They had to take it off! Chhouk is so cute. Well, that's what I think, and sorry to interrupt the story. So where was I? After they took his foot off, they made him a new one out of molded plastic. He uses a smooth sock just like Winter!

The real second-to-last animal is a turtle named Tonka. One of Tonka's legs got bit off by a dog. So Pennisula Humane Society workers got a toy wheel and put it on the turtle's shell. Suddenly Tonka was wheeling from place to place.

Last but not least, there is another dolphin named Fuji! Just like Winter she lost her tail! Fuji played with kids at the Okinawa Aquarium until a mysterious disease started eating her tail like a sandwich. Bridgestone Tire company (Wait one second, did you hear that? A tire company helped!) worked on a new rubber tail for Fuji. The first two tails did not work for her, just like Winter, but the third tail worked. There was a new sock made of silicone, rubber, and foam padding. That's all the animals! Hooray!

Now you've learned a lot about animal prosthetics—and most important, if you see an injured animal you can always help out by contacting a scientist. Hooray again!

Dear Dead People

JUAN BENITEZ ✳ *age 8*
Thomas Edison Charter Academy

The letter below first appeared in Look Closer/Mira de Cerca, *the chapbook published twice yearly in both English and Spanish that compiles the creative writing projects the students in our After-School Tutoring Program complete at the Writing Table.*

✳ ✳ ✳

Dear Dead People,

We are going to celebrate Día de los Muertos. Your memories are still with us; we can count on them. It does not matter if it's your family or not because it is still something sad. You might love or might not know them. Please don't worry because you can always do something to make yourself feel better.

Love Blah, Blah, Blah

JACKY CARRILLO * *age 12*
James Lick Middle School

This poem is from the fall 2012 edition of the annual sixth-grade poetry project at James Lick Middle School, when more than 200 sixth graders write poems with tutors from 826 Valencia in their on-campus Writers' Room.

* * *

Love is like pizza.
You add every topping
trying to make your customer happy.
They dislike it
like the smell of a hard rotten egg.
You feel like trash.

Love is like a dream
that turns into a nightmare.
You see everything in the color pink
and you love it.
Then everything turns black and scary.
Then you can never remember how good you felt
before the "dream."

Love is like a roller coaster.
You feel excited on the way up
and terrified on the way back down,
even though you think you have the guts
to go through anything.

Love is like a soda.
You open the can,
it's full of fizz, and it's delicious.
After some time,
it tastes plain (like water).

Remember, it isn't a game.
It's destiny.
Love can be amazing
depending on who you share it with.

Darkness Helping

JESSICA BERRIOS * *age 9*
Fairmount Elementary School

This play was created at the Writing Table during After-School Tutoring and first appeared in Look Closer/Mira de Cerca.

* * *

Darkness is walking through the woods, sad and depressed. It is thinking about how to be better.

Darkness I need to be a better thing, and I need to do it before morning. I will go to the village and try to be better.

Darkness walks to the village. He is thinking a lot of good things.

Darkness My instincts are tingling. Somebody is having a bad dream.

Darkness goes to the person's house and into the room of the person with nightmares.

Darkness Wake up, little girl!

Girl Who are you? Are you a ghost?

Darkness How can I help you?

Girl I am scared because I had a bad dream.

Darkness Just think good thoughts, and you will have good dreams.

Soon the girl is sleeping with good dreams. Darkness is happy to help.

The end.

Small Town Loves (Two Monologues)

ARTY ZHANG * *age 18*
Lowell High School

The following monologues were written during the Writing and Publishing Apprenctices workshop.

* * *

A MAN IN HIS MID-TWENTIES

My daughter had a nosebleed that wouldn't stop. And all I could do was drive her to the hospital, thinking of the ways that I couldn't help her. I would hold her, but your hands get so bloody from holding something you love.

I didn't know what to do. I barely finished high school. I didn't even want to, but my wife, Marian—she was pregnant at the time—told me to. I couldn't wait to get out—carry on the family legacy and all that. Back then, in Fremont, it was the ironworks, now it's the steel mill. And now it's empty. I was one of the first to be let go when the economy plummeted. You can carry on the family legacy, but the legacy can't carry you.

My daughter, when we got to hospital, was scared. Pale. She looked broken, the front of her clothes were all stained with blood. She was dizzy, not from blood loss, but from the sight of it. We didn't want her to look in the mirror, but she could see, from her reflection in the sliding glass doors, in people's shocked faces. In our faces. We couldn't blame her, we were dizzy too.

The doctor—he said that we had to pay. A lot. I didn't have insurance. It got expensive. I couldn't pay. And my daughter, between us. I could smell the blood, subtle, like the earth. It made me think. My father—his father fed him, clothed him, raised him with money from the ironworks. My father had iron blood in his veins. That's what he would tell us, and would tell us we had iron blood as well. He worked at the steel mill. He—he was so proud. We grew up from the same stuff he did. We—my family, this entire town, we were—are—all children of iron. That's how I fed my daughter too, from the steel mill. That's how she grew up.

My daughter's blood smells like iron. It was a mistake to bring her up—to make her in this way, shape her in my own image. There is no place in the world anymore for someone like that—for us. I'm obsolete. Not too old to die young, but a piece of the past. When the doctor told me that I had to—I realized—I couldn't do anything. There was nothing I could do.

[Pause]

We bleed iron, but all that matters is paper. When the bills come, and you open them, they are written in bloodred ink and they tell you that you are worth less than—worth less than the white sheet this is written on.

* * *

A YOUNG COLLEGE WOMAN, DISTRAUGHT

When you ask me why I left, you have to understand: I thought I wasn't leaving behind anything that mattered. Only the linoleum panels, only the stiff air of a small town sucking away at the years left in you. But you don't think about the people—well—you always think the people stay the same.

It must have been devastating when she—Annie—died. I didn't hear about it for a long time. When they told me, over the phone, they mentioned her mother. My aunt. I remembered her, sitting in the same chair and looking out the window. Every day after school I would babysit Annie, her daughter—my cousin.

My aunt's favorite phrase was, "God works in mysterious ways," and she blamed everything from tornadoes to the pennies under the couch on God. I don't think she ever understood why her husband left her. I don't think she ever forgave herself, but she had God to blame.

I thought about Annie sometimes, about how she could have grown up. She could have become a housewife or a bartender in equal measure, left behind. I wonder if she could have escaped. They say it was an accident; she wasn't even driving the car, but some part of me thinks she never had a chance.

God works in mysterious ways. And people leave. And sometimes you forgive them, but it's always easier to blame someone else. And when you leave… is there anyone you can blame? When I left—it wasn't like I could have taken her with me. Wasn't it?

She can't forgive me now, and when I think about her—when you leave—you always think the people stay the same.

And she was only a kid when I left.

Cake Me Up

ELLESSE GUTIERREZ ✳ *age 13*
James Lick Middle School

This piece is an example of a snapshot of words from the project "Snapshots" with Ms. Hacker and Ms. Babcock's seventh-grade students at James Lick Middle School.

* * *

The music blasted throughout the house. As my cousin Keianna and I started to feel the music, we rushed into the living room like Angelina Jolie adopting kids. Back then we loved being the center of attention, like Lady Gaga with her meat dress. On top of that, it was my birthday, so I thought to myself, I'm already the birthday girl, why not try and wear my mom's heels for the whole day? But we all know that didn't happen, and the day slowly faded away with my feet hurting and me being six.

Latina Girl from the Mission

ALEJANDRA MARTINEZ * *age 17*
John O'Connell High School

Over several weeks during the spring of 2012, the juniors in Ms. Leathers and Mr. Zwettler's classes at John O'Connell High School worked with 826 Valencia tutors to write and edit their essays on what it means to identify as a part of a group. The essays were originally published in a chapbook called From Me to We: Short Essays on Group Identity.

* * *

I am a young lady who grew up in the Mission neighborhood. Oftentimes, I have been misjudged by people who aren't too familiar with Latinas. They might think we are cholas (gangster girls) up to no good, troublemakers, getting pregnant at young ages, illegal aliens, gang members, the girlfriends of gangsters—the stereotypes can go on and on. Well, the sad truth is that here in the Mission, around 24th Street to be specific, we do have to face many of those things. But in reality we are not the stereotypes that people make us out to be.

Honestly, living in the Mission district I am surrounded with plenty of negative things. Some examples include violence, drugs, alcohol, and so on. I can't lie, I do have a couple of friends my age (maybe a year older or younger) with kids, but I'm seventeen years old and I'm here making it without a kid. I want to be someone. I want to do something with my life, get out of this environment. That's all my mom wants me to do—be successful. She tells me every day, she pushes me to do better in school, and she's always getting on me when she sees me messing up. She wants the best for me. She and my dad came to this country for a better life. They wanted the best for us, and they wanted to have better jobs to support us.

I have friends in similar situations and they want a better life for themselves. I have a friend that I'm really close to. She is eighteen years old, she's pregnant by her boyfriend, who is in a gang, and she's going through it all alone because he went to jail. Even though she's in a tough situation, she is still going to school at San Francisco State and she's not giving up school for anything. She also wants to do something with her life and not depend on anyone. That is just one of the stories of my friends who have defied the stereotypes surrounding Latina teenagers.

Yeah, there are some stereotypes that have been supported by statistics. For example, teen birth rates for Latinas in the Mission are fifty-five per one thousand births, higher than African-Americans. Of all the city neighborhoods, the Mission is one of the city's hot zone neighborhoods. According to the Mission Girls program website, 6 percent of eleventh graders report dating violence and 7 percent report forced sexual intercourse. That's only of the people that reported abuse—I believe that many people keep that to themselves. Thirty percent of babies born to a teen mom have a teen dad (the rest of the dads are over eighteen).

This one time I was in class and at my little table we were talking about college and stuff. Out of nowhere some white kid told me I wasn't going to be no one; he said I was just going to end up like all the other Latinas, either getting pregnant or just going to City College, dropping out and working at Chuck E. Cheese or something. He said it like it was cool and as if he didn't care. He meant it too. That got me mad, I felt offended.

I just acted like it was whatever and said, "All right, you will see then." I still don't like that kid. That fat, tall, white pimple-faced kid. His voice was nasally, and he walked with a hunched back. I still don't like him to this day.

Although the Mission is a "bad neighborhood," as some people put it, I love being from here. I love where I grew up. Most people expect and think the worst of us. Oftentimes, what people expect might actually happen. I believe the reason for this is that we are already born into a certain environment because our parents might be immigrants struggling to find jobs or might just be part of the cycle. Society set it up for us long ago—they set us up for failure. They like seeing other Latinas getting pregnant, dropping out, or joining gangs. They want to see it happen over and over again.

Sometimes some girls might be too sucked into it, trying to be the baddest, sickest girl out there. Or we hear it so much that we think that's the way it's supposed to be and it will never change, and the cycle just keeps going. Me, I'm going to break that cycle for myself. I'm going to be one of the few Latinas who becomes someone important with money. I know I will. I want to be a role model for Latina girls when I become somebody. I'm just getting started, and I won't give up.

When I'm Eighty

URIEL DELGADO * *age 7*
St. James School

One last word from the Writing Table of After-School Tutoring.

* * *

When I'm eighty years old, I'm still going to be strong.

You made it! You're probably thinking, "Phew! Now I know every single thing that happened at 826 Valencia in the last ten years. Nothing more to know." But you're wrong. There's more to know about everything, and there are more people and projects involved in a single week at 826 than we could fit in this entire book. If this were a multivolume affair, here we would list every volunteer who has ever tutored, edited, or taught at 826, but we've pretty much used up our page count already. So consider this the tip of the iceberg that makes 826 a grand glacier. Just imagine that for every name, publication, and program listed in the coming pages, there are a few hundred names of volunteers, too. This may sound fantastic, but you just finished reading the *826 Quarterly.* Your imagination should be pretty limbered up by now. ✱

About 826 Valencia

The People of 826 Valencia

THE STAFF OF 826 VALENCIA

Raúl Alcantar *Programs Coordinator*
Emilie Coulson *Director of Education*
Jorge Garcia *Programs Director*
Lauren Hall *Programs Director*
Randy Hyde *Director of Development*
Yalie Kamara *Volunteer and Internship Coordinator*
Olivia White Lopez *Pirate Store Manager*
María Inés Montes *Design Director*
Abner Morales *Interim Executive Director*
Molly Parent *Programs Assistant*
Valrie Sanders *Director of Finance and Operations*
Miranda Tsang *Communications Manager*

THE BELOVED INTERNS OF 826 VALENCIA
Winter/Spring 2013

Chelsea Brunetti	John Gibbs	Iris Lerch
Olivia Camenga	Sarah Griffin	Grant MacHamer
Carrie Clements	Emmanuelle	Pamela Martinez
Lila Cutter	Joyeux	Amanda Meth
Joy Ding	Brian Karfunkel	Sukhraj Sihota
Chris Ercolano	Joe Lash	Kayla Turner

THE 826 VALENCIA BOARD OF DIRECTORS

Michael Beckwith Olive Mitra   Andrew Strickman
Barb Bersche   Abner Morales   Vendela Vida
Thomas Mike   Mary Schaefer

826 VALENCIA CO-FOUNDERS

Nínive Calegari, Dave Eggers

HOW TO GET INVOLVED

What's that? You have some free time in your schedule that you don't know what to do with? Maybe it's time for you to join the crew aboard the HMS 826! We are always on the lookout for more volunteers to help us with our programming. Also, we can always use more volunteers with software skills, advanced editing skills, or advanced design skills. It's easy to become a volunteer and a bunch of fun to actually do it. Please fill out our online application to let us know you'd like to be a part of what we do:

826valencia.org/get-involved/volunteer

826 NATIONAL

826 Valencia's success has spread across the country. Under the umbrella of 826 National, writing and tutoring centers have opened up in seven more cities. If you would like to learn more about other 826 programs, please visit the following websites.

826 National	**826 DC**	**826 NYC**
826national.org	826dc.org	826nyc.org
826 Boston	**826 LA**	**826 Seattle**
826boston.org	826la.org	826seattle.org
826 CHI	**826 Michigan**	**826 Valencia**
826chi.org	826michigan.org	826valencia.org

The Programs of 826 Valencia

We are so proud of the student writing collected in this tenth-anniversary edition of the *826 Quarterly*. It is the result of countless hours of hard work by students and teachers alike. We are also endlessly inspired by our hardworking tutors, all of whom make the following programs possible. If you have not yet visited 826 Valencia, or if it has been a while, please do come by to see us—we'll treat you to a good mopping, free of charge.

AFTER-SCHOOL TUTORING

Five days a week, 826 Valencia is packed with students who come in for free one-on-one tutoring. Students receive help on their homework and then visit the Writing Table, where they tackle prompts around a monthly theme. We're particularly proud of our thriving services and support for young students learning English and our high school–specific hours in the evenings.

FIELD TRIPS

Three or four times a week, 826 Valencia welcomes an entire class of students for a morning of high-energy learning. Classes may request a custom-designed curriculum on a subject they've been studying, such as playwriting, or choose from one of our five field-trip plans. Our most popular is the Storytelling & Bookmaking field trip. In two hours, the students write, illustrate, and publish their own books. They leave with keepsake stories and a newfound excitement for writing.

IN-SCHOOLS PROGRAMMING

826 Valencia's in-school programming reaches the greatest number of students as we go into public schools across the city to support teachers with their curricula and give students individualized attention. While collaborating with teachers on their programs, tutors help students with the expository and creative writing inherent to each project.

WORKSHOPS

826 Valencia offers workshops almost every day of the year at the 826 writing lab. Workshops are devoted to teaching a variety of skills including but not limited to comics, podcasting, and personal statements for high school seniors. They are taught by professionals in the literary arts in classes of twelve to fifteen students, so each student gets the individual attention he or she needs. At the end of the workshop, the students' work is read live to an audience at 826, recorded and put online, made into a short film, or, most often, made into a fine chapbook that each student gets to keep and that we sell in our store.

SUMMER PROGRAMS

During the summer, our tutoring program caters to elementary school students who are reading and writing below grade level. Our project-based curriculum focuses on boosting literacy skills and confidence over six weeks of activities. We also host an intensive writing camp for high school students in which campers write all day, every day, and work with celebrated authors and artists such as Michael Chabon, ZZ Packer, and Spike Jonze.

WRITERS' ROOMS

Our Writers' Rooms at Everett Middle School and James Lick Middle School are beautiful in-school satellites, decorated in the style of 826, where our volunteers tutor nearly every student in the school over the course of the year. Teachers send half their class to the Writers' Rooms to receive one-on-one attention on writing assignments while they focus on a smaller class size in their own rooms.

The Publications of 826 Valencia

826 Valencia produces a variety of publications in addition to the *826 Quarterly,* each of which contains work written by students in our various programs. Some are professionally printed and nationally distributed; others are glued together here and sold in the pirate store. These projects represent some of the most exciting work at 826 Valencia, as they enable Bay Area students to experience a world of publishing not otherwise available to them. Students of 826 wrote for the following publications:

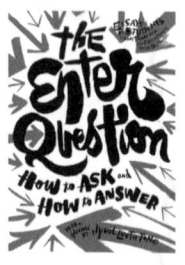

The Enter Question: How to Ask and How to Answer (2013) is a collection of essays on issues of immigrant identity written by the eleventh-grade class at San Francisco International High School. Each of these young authors, most of whom are new speakers and writers of English, worked intensively with our tutors to pen essays that share their story with the world. The stories here deal with starting life in a new country, remembering one's home and retaining and adapting traditions, and issues faced by all teenagers as they struggle to forge identity and community. With a forward by Nyuol Lueth Tong, this is a deeply moving collection, touching on universal themes in more than eighty distinct voices.

Arrive, Breathe, and Be Still (2012) In this collection by thirty-five students at Downtown High School in San Francisco, and with a foreword by playwright Octavio Solis, the young writers explore the themes of resistance and resilience through their original monologues and plays. After a semester of working intensely with actors at American Conservatory Theater and writing tutors from 826 Valencia, the students produced this powerful look into the realities of high school life, the pressures surrounding young people, and the strength it takes to keep going. Perfect for reading or performing, these pieces are a refreshing tool for using theater both in the classroom and outside of it.

Beyond Stolen Flames, Forbidden Fruit, and Telephone Booths (2011) is a collection of essays and short stories, written by fifty-three juniors and seniors at June Jordan School for Equity, in which young writers explore the role of myth in our world today. Students wrote pieces of fiction and nonfiction, retelling old myths, creating new ones, celebrating everyday heroes, and recognizing the tales that their families have told over and over. With a foreword by Khaled Hosseini, the result is a collection with a powerful message about the stories that have shaped students' perspectives and the world they know.

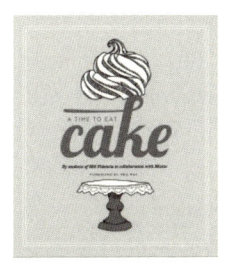

A Time to Eat Cake (2011) is a collection of short pieces from the students in 826 Valencia's after-school tutoring program. In collaboration with San Francisco pastry shop Miette, students spent a month exploring memories, imagining their ideal treats, and spinning amazing tales of cake adventures. With a foreword by Miette founder Meg Ray, this book shows that you don't have to be Proust to know the power of sweets.

We the Dreamers (2010) is a collection of essays by fifty-one juniors at John O'Connell High School reflecting on what the American Dream means to them. The students recount stories about family, home, immigration, hardship, and the hopes of their generation — as well as those of the generation that raised them. The result is a firsthand account of these essayists' often-complicated relationship with our national ethos that is insightful, impassioned, surprising, and of utmost importance to our understanding of what the American Dream means for their generation.

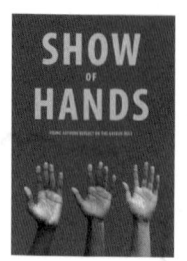

Show of Hands (2009) is a collection of stories and essays written by fifty-four juniors and seniors at Mission High School. It amplifies the students' voices as they reflect on one of humanity's most revered guides for moral behavior: the Golden Rule, which tells us that we should act toward others as we would want them to act toward us. Whether speaking about global issues, street violence, or the way to behave among friends and family, the voices of these young essayists are brilliant, thoughtful, and, most of all, urgent.

Thanks and Have Fun Running the Country (2009) is a collection of letters penned by our after-school tutoring students to newly elected President Obama. In this collection, which arrived at inauguration time, there's loads of advice for the president, often hilarious, sometimes heartfelt, and occasionally downright practical. The letters have been featured in the *New York Times,* the *San Francisco Chronicle,* and on *This American Life.*

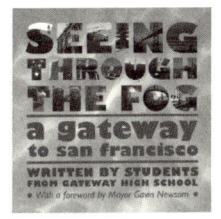

Seeing Through the Fog (2008) is a guidebook written by seniors from Gateway High School that explores San Francisco from tourist, local, and personal perspectives. Both whimsical and factually accurate, the pieces in this collection take the reader to the places that teenagers know best, from taquerias to skate spots to fashionable shops that won't break your budget.

Exactly (2007) is a hardbound book of colorful stories for children, ages nine to eleven. This collection of fifty-six narratives by students at Raoul Wallenberg Traditional High School is illustrated by forty-three professional artists. It passes on lessons that teenagers want the next generation to know.

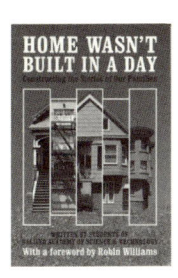

Inspired by magical realism, students at Galileo Academy of Science and Technology produced *Home Wasn't Built in a Day* (2006), a collection of short stories based on family myths and legends. With a foreword by actor and comedian Robin Williams, the book comes alive through powerful student voices that explore just what it is that makes a house a home.

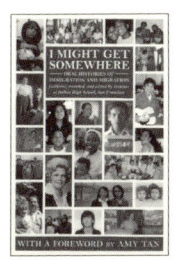

I Might Get Somewhere: Oral Histories of Immigration and Migration (2005) exhibits an array of student-recorded oral narratives about moving to San Francisco from other parts of the United States and all over the world. Acclaimed author Amy Tan wrote the foreword to this compelling collection of personal stories by Balboa High School students. All these narratives shed light on the problems and pleasures of finding one's life in new surroundings.

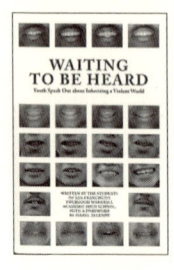

Written by thirty-nine students at Thurgood Marshall Academic High School, *Waiting to Be Heard: Youth Speak Out About Inheriting a Violent World* (2004) addresses violence and peace on a personal, local, and global scale. With a foreword by Isabel Allende, the book combines essays, fiction, poetry, and experimental writing to create a passionate collection of student expression.

Talking Back: What Students Know About Teaching (2003) is a book that delivers the voices of the class of 2004 from Leadership High School. In reading the book—previously a required-reading textbook at San Francisco State University and Mills College—you will understand the relationships students want with their teachers, how students view classroom life, and how the world affects students.

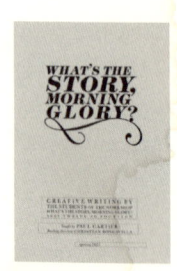

826 Valencia also publishes scores of chapbooks each semester. These collections of writing primarily come from two sources: our volunteer-taught evening and weekend workshops, and our in-school projects, where students work closely with tutors to edit their writing. Designed and printed right at 826 Valencia, the resulting chapbooks range from student-penned screenplays to collections of bilingual poetry.

PUBLICATIONS FOR STUDENTS & TEACHERS

Don't Forget to Write (2005) contains fifty-four of the best lesson plans used in workshops taught at 826 Valencia, 826NYC, and 826LA, giving away all of our secrets for making writing fun. Each lesson plan was written by its original workshop teacher, including Jonathan Ames, Aimee Bender, Dave Eggers, Erika Lopez, Julie Orringer, Jon Scieszka, Sarah Vowell, and many others. If you are a parent or a teacher, this book is meant to make your life easier, as it contains enthralling and effective ideas to get your students writing. It can also be used as a resource for the aspiring writer. In 2011, 826 National published a two-volume second edition of *Don't Forget to Write,* also available in our pirate supply store.

The Store at 826 Valencia

"Definitely one of the top five pirate stores I've been to recently." — DAVID BYRNE

What happens in the store at 826 Valencia? Many have said that upon entering San Francisco's only independent pirate supply store, they get a sensation of déjà vu. Others walk in and feel at once the miracle work of an unseen hand. And there are those whose eyes bulge and shrink simultaneously, their thoughts so convoluted that they are unable to shout or mutter the question that most plagues them: "What is this place?"

PIRATE STORE STAFF & VOLUNTEERS

Pirate Store Staff
Chris Gomez
Caroline Kangas
Olivia White Lopez
Joel Morley
Byron Weiss

Window Display Artists
Lisa Brown
Justin Carder
Caroline Kangas
Amy Langer
Paul Madonna
Tatiana Pavlova
Otis Pig
Tim Ratanapreukskul

With ten years under our silk sashes, we naturally have a lot of advice to share with the pillage-and-plundering community. Namely, try not to bring your finest of frilly lace cuffs aboard ship, unless you're okay with them turning pink in the wash. Also: Never scrape the bottom of the gruel pot with a wooden spoon—it's unbecoming.

Below we have culled from the experiences of our sophisticated, albeit salty, seafaring clientele to provide the most up-to-date advice on how to keep life aboard ship shipshape. Read on for advice on how *not* to dress your new wooden leg and the proper gift-giving etiquette within the aquatic life in-crowd. Perhaps you're currently nervous about that first sword fight? Or you're an old-timer who is out of practice and just looking to brush up on the basics? Well, lucky for you, our newest pirate supplier, Lord Byron, has got you covered. This compendium will be especially helpful to those newly dedicating themselves to a life at sea.

* * *

WELL KNOWN SEA PROVERBS

Scurvy-ridden Larry is as scurvy-ridden Larry does.

Finders keepers, losers weepers—except if the quartermaster finds out that you took something that wasn't yours and then you lose a hand.

A good parrot is hard to find.

A man of the sea is a man indeed.

A man who eats another man is no man indeed.

Keep your powder monkeys dry.

Hard tack springs eternal.

A fish in the hand is worth a high five.

Jake is the captain's best friend.

Prisms are pretty but diamonds are a girl's best friend.

There are always more dolphins in the sea.

What can't be cured must be eaten very quickly.

You can't jump into the water and expect to become a fish.

A siren cannot change its song.

You can't raise a sail without putting yourself in danger of being tickled by that prank-playing gunner.

A leg saved is a leg earned.

Put a leech on it.

* * *

FASHION DON'TS FOR YOUR NEW WOODEN LEG
Otis Pig

- DON'T use spray-on wood polish. It gunks.
- DON'T paint the wood to match your skin tone. Tanning season can be so unpredictable.
- DON'T make fancy carvings in the wood unless you've really thought about how the design is going to reflect on you twenty or thirty years down the road.
- DON'T attend any beach bonfires for the first couple of months if the attendants will be drinking.
- DON'T give your new leg a nickname. Do NOT name it Peggy.
- DON'T wear wooden clogs, unless they complement the wood of your leg.
- DON'T attach bullet-hole stickers to the wood.
- DON'T forget to restain every four to six months.
- DON'T wear a sock over your leg. There's just no reason for it.
- DON'T let your wooden leg turn into a bulletin board. Pinning a few reminders up here and there is fine, but DON'T let it get tacky.
- DON'T glue hairs onto your leg. That's basically a comb-over and you know it.

For those unfamiliar with water-world etiquette, our intrepid reporter Caroline Kangas has gone straight to the source by interviewing the talented—and pleasantly gelatinous—jellyfish Celine (no last name, thank you) to find out how to shop for the-impossible-to-shop-for people in your life.

* * *

INTERVIEWS IN THE OCEAN
Caroline Kangas, *Daily Tide* **Reporter**
Jellyfish are not normally known for their generosity. Celine's family was no different; robbers and thieves, the lot of them. However, from a young age Celine sought a new course. Early in her life, she began to do favors for fellow jellies in need, and she would even leave small tokens for the other fish in their neck of the sea. As she continued growing, her tentacles could touch those even farther away, but she could only reach so many. Celine was addicted to the thrill of generosity but needed the help of others to spread joy to everyone in the world. A jellyfish of many talents, she used her skill of teaching to instruct others in effective benevolence. Most recently she took a position in our very own store window and I asked her for a few tips for those of us less "gifted" in the ways of giving…

Celine Suggests: A Gift-Giving Guide from our Resident Benevolent Jellyfish
Married to a lady who's married to the sea? Got a set of twin starfish to appease? Never know what to buy that hard-to-shop-for sunfish or seahorse? Is giving to one fish in the school but not the others practical or a faux pas?

The Sunfish, or a utilitarian type: Some people only understand utility. SeaHose are one perfect gift for these types: warm, comfortable, and stylish too!

The School of Fish, or all of your office coworkers: Want to buy a gift for a large group but don't want to break the bank?

Easy! A thoughtful card and a small trinket (think mini dice) show you care and help you stay in budget.

The Twin Starfish, or your friend's kids (or your own): When giving to kids (especially siblings), try to buy the same or similar for both or there are bound to be fights. Treasure chests are safe for all ages and you can continue adding to them in the future. (A fine investment.)

The Turtle, or the homebody: Have any friends who carry their home with them? Well, then give them something to decorate their favorite place! Add a little sparkle with a Luxury-Size Deck Prism.

The Crab, or your crabby sister who never likes anything you buy her: Try to get in touch with the gift recipient's interests. Does this person live in the sea? Do they like the sea? Are they a sea animal? Well, boy, howdy, we bet she'd enjoy the fine McSweeney's Publication *Animals of the Ocean*.

The Seahorse, or the dramatist in your life: Know someone who can never break out of character? Perhaps that friend of yours who speaks in iambic pentameter? Give him an eye patch so he can fully commit to his belief that all the world's a stage.

You: Remember, at the end of the day it's okay to treat yourself, too! As captain of the ship you might consider buying yourself a hook, now even more reasonably priced at $299.99.

* * *

SWORDFIGHTING TIPS
Byron Weiss

When fighting at sea, most battles are decided by who has the most cannons. However, in the event of hand-to-hand combat, being skilled with a blade will mean the difference between victory and walking the plank. Here are a few guidelines to heed when handling a sword:

1. Always hold your weapon at the hilt.
2. Keep your point trained on your target.
3. Flourishing, while impressive, usually ends in the loss of limbs.
4. Practice with both hands. (You never know when you might lose one.)
5. Some sand or a spare knife in an off hand can prove useful in a pinch.
6. Parrots can be trained to fight as well as talk.
7. Don't cross blades if you can win through easier methods.
8. Never give up the high ground.
9. Keep an eye patch handy. Again, *you never know.*

It's Always a Good Time to Give

Whether it's loose change or heaps of cash, a donation of any size will help 826 Valencia continue to offer a wide variety of FREE literacy and publishing programs to Bay Area youths. We would greatly appreciate your support.

Please make a donation at:
826valencia.org/get-involved/donate
You can also mail your contribution to:
826 Valencia Street, San Francisco, California 94110

Your donation is tax deductible. What a plus! Thank you!

826 VALENCIA & THE 826 QUARTERLY

would be so very proud to publish your short story, poem, essay, movie script, stage play, dramatic monologue, haiku, interview, or anything you have written, care about, and want to share with the world. But in order to publish your work, you must...

Submit!

PUBLISH YOUR WORK IN THE *826 QUARTERLY*!

PROVE FRIENDS AND FAMILY **Wrong!**

OR PROVE THEM **Right!**

(DEPENDING ON WHAT THEY'VE BEEN SAYING)

Young authors who live all across the United States, have you written a short story, long story, novella, poem, play, script, essay, memoir, particularly poignant laundry list, etc.? We want to read your work! We urge you, if you're under eighteen years of age and have written something you are proud of, to submit your work for publication. It could appear in our very next issue!

E-mail Submissions to
826quarterly@gmail.com

Be Sure to Include
your full name, your age, where you're from, the name of the school you attend, and your contact information

If You Prefer Regular Mail
our address is:
826 Valencia Street, San Francisco, California 94110

✱ DON'T LET THIS CHANCE PASS YOU BY! ✱